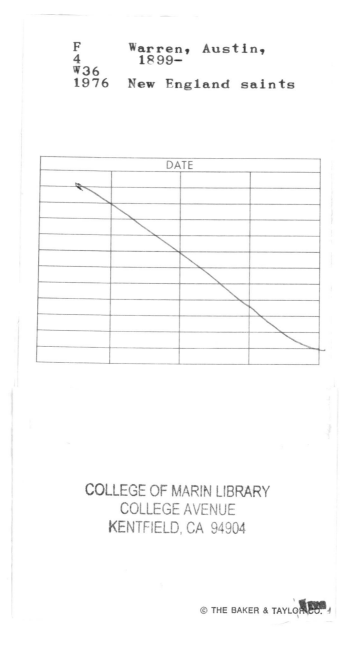

NEW ENGLAND SAINTS

New England Saints

AUSTIN WARREN

GREENWOOD PRESS, PUBLISHERS
WESTPORT, CONNECTICUT

Library of Congress Cataloging in Publication Data

Warren, Austin, 1899-
   New England saints.

   Reprint of the 1956 ed. published by University
of Michigan Press, Ann Arbor.
   Bibliography: p. ·
   1. New England--Intellectual life. 2. Religious thought--New England. I. Title.
[F4.W36   1976]   209'.74   76-28302
ISBN 0-8371-9086-X

Originally published in 1956 by The University of Michigan Press,
Ann Arbor

Reprinted with the permission of The University of Michigan Press

Reprinted in 1976 by Greenwood Press,
a division of Williamhouse-Regency Inc.

Library of Congress Catalog Card Number 76-28302

ISBN 0-8371-9086-X

Printed in the United States of America

FOREWORD

There are two strains in the New England character: the Yankee trader and the Yankee saint (often a complex of scholar, priest, and poet).

This book is devoted to the saints. The Puritans, like St. Paul, used that term to designate members of their church, communicants, 'the elect.' I have used it more widely, but with a definite criterion. My saints are, none of them, canonized; but they are, whether priests, and of whatever 'communion,' men I recognize, and celebrate, as those to whom reality was the spiritual life, whose spiritual integrity was their calling and vocation. This is a hagiography, designed, like all hagiographies, for instruction, to be sure, but primarily for edification: "Wherefore seeing we are compassed about with so great a cloud of witnesses, . . . let us run with patience the race that is set before us."

The chapters give examples from four centuries of New England's spiritual life and with some adequacy represent the spiritual movements of those centuries: the Puritans of the seventeenth century; the Edwardean 'Scholastics' of the eighteenth century; the Transcendentalism of the early nineteenth century and its counterstatement, overlapping the century mark, of proto- and neo-humanism; in the last essay, the unnamed movement of which F. O. Matthiessen and John Wheelwright were at once martyrs and saints.

CONTENTS

NEW ENGLAND SAINTS

THE PURITAN POETS

The characteristics of the New England character and mind have remained conspicuously constant from the seventeenth century to the present. The character is lean and angular, firm and steadfast but ungracious. It owed obedience first to the God of Abraham, Isaac, and Jacob; then to Duty, "stern daughter of the voice of God," with conscience as relentless director. Its mind is shrewd in its lower ranges, speculative in its upper. It respects erudition. Wrote Edward Johnson, of Harvard's foundation: "After God had carried us safe to New England, and we had builded our houses, provided necessaries for our livelihood, reared convenient places for God's worship, and settled the civil government, one of the next things we longed for and looked after was to advance learning and perpetuate it to our posterity, dreading to leave an illiterate ministry to the Churches, when our present ministers shall lie in the dust."

If New England has sometimes, with Emerson, attacked the achievements of the memory, the motive has been fear of the ancestral temptation. But the New Englander takes naturally to nonconformity and scepticism of ritual, and, like Emerson's or John Wheelwright's, his learning lies more readily in Platonism, or the Sacred Books of the East, or the Apocryphal gospels, than in the classical tradition.

Not a very sensuous creature either in life or in art, the New Englander is rarely incited to listen to the dark blood or to indeed imagine that it could teach him anything worth the attention of an honest man. In place of intuition or instinct, he trusts to calculation: he "calates" (that is, calculates) his action. Not animality but cerebralism is his characteristic vice; and he is far more readily a crank than a libertine.

The natural consequence of his mind and his character makes him an inevitable teacher, academically accredited or not. Till well after the Civil War, the New Englanders were, literally, schoolmasters of the nation; they were also — through the writings of Cummington, Concord, Cambridge, and Boston — the literary inciters to the good life. Poe, by comic accident born in Boston, named the New England literary mode the "heresy of the didactic." There have been apparent exceptions like that earnest propagandist and loyal fighter Amy Lowell; but the New England tradition still speaks through Robert Lowell and John Wheelwright. To his *Political Self-Portrait* Wheelwright appended: "This book, an essay in bringing good men forth, being intended for lasting entertainment, is didactic . . . The main point is not what noise poetry makes, but how it makes you think

4

and act, — not what you make of it, but what it makes of you."

The New England of which we are now to speak is the Puritan Massachusetts Bay Colony, with Harvard College as its thesaurus of learning, sound doctrine, and polite letters. The Tenth Muse, as a female, was necessarily without benefit of a collegiate education; but the male poets of the century were all Harvard men — and all, with the exception of Tompson, who became a schoolmaster, clergymen.

We know now that Milton was not an isolated humanist among Psalm-singing bigots; that the Puritans had no objection to the organ and other musical instruments — except in the meeting house; that, doctrinally, they were not genuine Calvinists but held the more liberal "Covenant Theology" of William Ames; that as thinkers, they followed the logical and rhetorical methods of Ramus, the progressive critic and simplifier of what passed for Aristotelianism; that Harvard College, which inculcated the "purest phrase of Terence and Erasmus" and taught the Greek pastoral and elegiac poets as well as the Hebrew Testament, aimed at more than a divinity curriculum; and that the Puritans were restricted in the practice of the arts far more by the labor of frontier enterprise than by any theoretical hostility.

Libraries were chiefly classical and theological; but John Harvard's collection, brought with him from England, included Wither's poems and Quarles'. Governor Dudley, Anne Bradstreet's father, owned a copy of *Piers Plowman.*

The Reverend Increase Mather read the poems of George Herbert as well as Herbert's *Country Parson.* A Boston bookseller's invoice of 1683 names, along with

5

a copy of Sidney's *Arcadia*, two copies of Rochester's *Poems* as well as Burnett's account of the rake's pious end, and four copies of *Paradise Lost*. Several "common-place books," compiled by Harvard students, have come down to us, the most engaging that of Elnathan Chauncy, son of the President and undergraduate in the 1660's. Chauncy copied out lyrics from Herrick's *Hesperides*, Cleveland's "Song of Mark Antony," stanzas from Joseph Beaumont's *Psyche* (1648) and Warner's *Albions England;* and he filled more than twenty closely written pages with quotations from Spenser, giving the *Shepheardes Calendar* almost in its entirety.

With the Restoration, England moved into a new literary world, of which — according to the verdict of Dr. Johnson — Waller and Denham were the discoverers and Dryden the primate. Politically, theologically, and morally out of sympathy with the age which followed the breakdown of their hopes, the New Englanders took little interest in the literature which was its product. Even *Paradise Lost*, published in 1667, had no influence upon New England verse till well into the eighteenth century. If, for English literary history, the seventeenth century breaks, about 1660, into sharply contrasting periods — "metaphysical" and "neoclassical" — for American literary history the century forms a unit, and the new mode is delayed till the age of Anne. It is with the Reverend Mather Byles and Dr. Franklin that Boston becomes neoclassical.

The masterpiece — the epic — of Puritan poetry for seventeenth century New Englanders was not *Paradise Lost* but a work which in some measure influenced it — the *Divine Weekes*, Joshua Sylvester's translation from the French of the Huguenot nobleman Du Bartas, published in 1605. The first of Du Bartas' weeks is the week

6

of creation. For length and elaboration it exceeds Book VII of *Paradise Lost* in proportion, as that in turn exceeds the ancestral treatment in Genesis. The Second Week, substantially a chronicle of Old Testament history, stands in a somewhat similar relation to Books XI and XII of Milton's epic. In style, Du Bartas was Baroque, not classical — a poet endlessly fertile in 'conceits' of the physical order, a master of what Addison was to call "false wit." He called the head the lodging of the understanding, the eyes the twin stars, the nose the "gutter" or "chimney," the teeth a double palisade used as a mill to the open throat.

The other poets from whom our New Englanders induced their theory of poetry are few. Anne Bradstreet's "Contemplations" uses the precise variant of the Spenserian stanza devised by Phineas Fletcher for his *Purple Island*. The poems of George Herbert and Francis Quarles were models for religious lyrics; and Quarles's *Samson* appears to have provided Tompson with the narrative style of his *New England's Crisis*.

A common characteristic of Du Bartas, Quarles, and Herbert is that, in their several ways, they are all masters of Baroque wit writing. In English literary history we are likely to think of Donne and "metaphysical poetry"; but we need a larger term to describe the whole movement of which Donne's dialectical, psychological, casuistic poetry is but one species. When these poets are religious, their style, with its metaphorical couplings between the normally disjunct, seems not merely a technic and certainly not a trick but an appropriate expression of their belief in a universe whose reality is not mechanical or sensible but personal and miraculous.

Both in old England and New, the Puritans were

7

favorers of the simple, unfigured manner of preaching, in opposition to the Anglo-Catholic splendor of Andrewes, Donne, and Jeremy Taylor. But the sermon, addressed to all sorts and conditions of men, must instruct all save the simplest hearers. In certain kinds of poetry this restriction to real universality seems not to have been operative.

No New England Puritan — with the exception of Edward Taylor and with the possible exception of Cotton Mather (whose Baroque *Magnalia*, published just at the end of the century, is a treasury of ingenuities)— had wit enough to rival the conceits of Du Bartas, Herbert, and Quarles. Save for their pentameter couplets and their panoramic scope, Anne Bradstreet's long poems have nothing in common with Du Bartas; she does not or cannot imitate his conceits:

> But when my wondering eyes and envious heart
> Great *Bartas* sugar'd lines, do but read o're
> Fool I do grudg the Muses did not part
> Twixt him and me that overfluent store;
> A *Bartas* can do what a *Bartas* will
> But simple I according to my skill.

The humbler ingenuities were what the New Englanders could reproduce. The anagram and its cognate forms, the acrostic and the chronogram, were favorite forms of clerical wit — here, as in old England, where the learned Camden had written an essay upon the genre, often accompanied by a verse epigram. In his elegy upon John Wilson, first pastor of the Boston Church, Cotton Mather writes of his

> Care to guide his flock, and feed his lambs,
> By words, works, prayers, psalms, alms, and anagrams:

8

THE PURITAN POETS

Those anagrams, in which he made to start
Out of mere nothings, by creating out
Whole words of counsel; did to motes unfold
Names, till they lessons gave richer than gold. . . .

Out of the letters composing the name "Anna Brade-
streate," the minister of Ipswich, Nathaniel Ward, "Simple Cobbler of Agawam," drew the significant rear-
rangements "Deer neat An Bartas" and "Artes bred neat
An," and husbanded these perceptions in the couplet:

So *Bartas* like thy fine spun Poems been,
That *Bartas* name will prove an Epicene.

Equally permissible was the edifying use of the pun.
The Reverend John Norton's elegy upon "That Pattern
and Patron of Virtue, the Truely Pious, Peerless, &
Matchless Gentlewoman, Mrs. Anne Bradstreet," so
develops its theme:

Her breast was a brave Pallace, a *Broad-street*,
Where all heroick ample thoughts did meet,
Where nature such a Tenement had tane,
That others souls, to hers, dwelt in a lane . . .

Another genre acceptable to the New England Puritan was the long instructive poem. Though it might be
narrative in form, the narrative must not be invented.
It might be secular history — like Anne Bradstreet's long
poem on the "Four Monarchies" (Assyrian, Persian,
Grecian, and Roman), which she based largely on Sir
Walter Raleigh's *History* and Archbishop Ussher's
Annals of the World — or like John Wilson's *Song of
Deliverance*, which tells, with edifying intercalations,
the story of England's triumphs over the wicked Papists
from the destruction of the Armada through the foiling
of the Gunpowder Plot and the death of the Catholics

9

gathered at Blackfriars. Benjamin Tompson's *New Englands Crisis* (1675) is a history of King Philip's War, with a prologue suggesting that the invasion of the Indians is retribution for the colony's increasing luxury, its lapse from the austere and democratic virtue of the founding fathers:

> Plain Tom and Dick would pass as current now
> As ever since 'Your Servant, Sir' and bow.
> Deep-skirted doublets, puritanic capes,
> Which now would render men like upright apes,
> Were comelier wear, our wiser fathers thought
> Than the cast fashions from all Europe brought.
> Twas in those days an honest grace would hold
> Till an hot pudding grew at heart a cold,
> And men had better stomachs at religion
> Than I to capon, turkey-cock, or pigeon . . .

Or it might be based upon the Bible, like *The Day of Doom* and "God's Determinations." The former, which was accompanied by marginal proof-texts from Holy Scripture, was written by the clergyman of Malden, the Reverend Michael Wigglesworth, during a period when, afflicted by a mysterious malady and unable to preach, he sought another means of serving the cause of religion. He put his terrifying picture of the Last Judgment into the old fourteeners, the meter of the popular ballads; and, after the manner of the popular "Nut Brown Maid," he made his poem the more obviously tuneful and the easier to memorize by supplying his long couplets with internal rhyme:

> They rush from Beds with giddy heads and to their
>   windows run,
> Viewing this light, which shines more bright than doth
>   the Noon-day Sun.

Straightway appears (they see't with tears) the Son of
  God most dread;
Who with his Train comes on amain to Judge both
  Quick and Dead.

The poem was memorized by many persons; it was reprinted in England; and, before 1828, it went through
fourteen editions; but it should probably not be thought
of as representing New England's own notion of her
best. It is upon grounds of wide popular edification that
Cotton Mather appears to praise it, when he remarks
of Wigglesworth that in his compositions "he proposed the Edification of such readers as are for plain
Truths dressed up in a Plain Meeter. The Composures
have had their Acceptance and Advantage among that
sort of Readers . . . "

"God's Determinations," by Edward Taylor, might
with tolerable accuracy be called a closet drama. The
concettist method, with its constant metaphysical explo-
sion, is scarcely adapted to the continuum of the epic or
the dramatic, but the poem can be read with persistent
interest.

And, last of the long poems, there is a delightful work
of Anne Bradstreet's, written before she was thirty, a
work which has no composite name, but which might
be called "A Quartet of Fours." It links together the
Four Elements (Fire, Air, Earth, and Water), the Four
Humours (Choler, Blood, Melancholy, Phlegm), the
Four Ages of Man (Childhood, Youth, Maturity, and
Old Age), and the Four Seasons. Each personification
speaks in turn, boasting his prowess and setting forth his
superiority to the other members of his group. The
structure, reminiscent of the English moralities and inter-
ludes, has its neat continuity. "The Four Ages of Man"

opens by relating its figures genealogically to the preceding quartets:

> Lo now four others act upon the stage,
> Childhood and Youth, the Manly, and Old Age,
> The first son unto phlegm, Grandchild to water,
> Unstable, supple, cold, and moist's his nature,
> The second, frolick, claims his pedigree
> From blood and air, for hot and moist is he.
> The third of fire and choler is composed
> Vindictive and quarrelsome disposed.
> The last of earth and heavy melancholy
> Solid, hating all lightness and all folly.

Then there are the Puritan lyrics. These do not assail the recalcitrant mistress with the pining lover's sighs, nor compare her charms to roses, lilies, and the stars. Puritan love is married love; and when we look to find the Puritan affectionately human we turn to the tender letters between John Winthrop and his second wife or to the widowed Sewall's addresses to Madame Winthrop or to his wife's biography of Colonel Hutchinson.

Anne Bradstreet, who composed her best poetry after *The Tenth Muse* (1650) was published in London, wrote charmingly of her children and her husband as well as of her Saviour. It was while Governor Bradstreet was in England on business for the Colony that she composed her punning poem in which three analogies, separately developed, are terminally united:

> As loving Hind that (Hartless) wants her Deer,
> Scuds through the woods and Fern with harkning ear,
> Perplext, in every bush and nook doth pry,
> Her dearest Deer, might answer ear or eye;
> So doth my anxious soul, which now doth miss,
> A dearer Dear (far dearer Heart) than this.

Two other lyrics of hers, "The Flesh and the Spirit" and "Contemplations," are undeniable poetry. The former, reminiscent of medieval colloquies between body and soul, begins admirably . . .

> In secret place where once I stood
> Close by the Banks of *Lacrim* flood
> I heard two sisters reason on
> Things that are past and things to come . . .

The latter is a meditation poem in the neo-Spenserian stanza of Phineas Fletcher. The formula is a familiar one: natural objects — the oak, the sun, the heavens, the elm, the river, the birds — all of which suggest some lesson applicable, by way of reproof, example, or emulation, to man. This is a formula which will fit many poems by Herbert, Vaughan, Wordsworth, and Bryant. The best pieces in which man superimposes himself, as exegete or disciple, upon the landscape, are those eschewing instruction mechanically deduced: those, indeed, written by medieval or Oriental minds, for whom analogy is but a literary version of the structure of the universe.

In "Contemplations," Mrs. Bradstreet was an emblemist: she looked at Nature before she looked through it; and she took delight in what she saw before she minded what it could teach; and, like Emily of Amherst, she was moved by the little and the obscure as well as the grandiose:

> I heard the merry grasshopper then sing,
> The blackclad Cricket bear a second part,
> They kept one tune and played on the same string,
> Seeming to glory in their little art . . .

Prevailingly serene and sunlit — an Epiphany of God in Nature, the poem gains in depth by the somber interlude in which the ever-present thought of Adam's Fall blots out the sunlight, and most of all by the solemn closing stanza with its allusion to that mysterious verse from Revelation — to the White Stone, the new name:

O Time, the fatal wrack of mortal things
That draws oblivions curtains over kings,
Their sumptuous monuments men know them not,
Their names without a record are forgot,
Their parts, their ports, their pomp's all laid in th'dust
Nor wit nor gold, nor buildings scape Time's rust;
But he whose name is grav'd in the white stone
Shall last and shine when all of these are gone.

But seventeenth-century New England 'wit' — still inclusive of 'fancy' and 'imagination' — appeared most inevitably in the funeral elegy. The chief occasion when the arts might be practiced as a pious duty was the death of some friend, relative, or eminent person. Then a funeral elegy was appropriate not only for addition to the memorial stone but, at more ambitious length, for circulation as appended to the biography or printed as a black-bordered broadside. Even in communities where existence is hard, death must have its luxuries: the humblest man deserves his moment of dignity, while the eminent divines and Colonial governors should be contemplated at length, that their examples of virtue, sagacity, and courage may be considered and appropriated.

The New England elegy was amusingly satirized by the youthful Benjamin Franklin in one of his Dogood letters to the *N. E. Courant* (1722). His recipe prescribes: "For the subject of your elegy: Take one of your neighbors who has lately departed this life. It is of no great matter at what age the party died, but it will be best if he went away suddenly, being killed, drowned, or frozen to death. Having chosen the person, take all his virtues, excellencies, etc.; and if he have not enough, you may borrow some to make up a sufficient quantity." But the New England elegy, as written by its experts, was rarely dull. More frequently, it prompted devout ingenuity. Since nothing in the life of a good man could be unordained by Providence, one's name — either in its pristine simplicity, or anagrammatically rearranged — or the disease one suffered from, or one's profession, or the mode of one's death: all were motifs not adventitious.

Cotton Mather, commemorating the Reverend Ralph Partridge, in the *Magnalia*, finds a life in a name: the Plymouth divine, defenseless by beak or claw, was hunted from his home by the ecclesiastical setters of the Old World, pursued to his covert on these shores, whence he took wings to become a bird of Paradise. His prose has its counterparts in the verses of the Reverend Nicholas Noyes (B.A., Harvard, 1667), whose elegy on the Reverend Joseph Green — the "green and growing olive tree" — is matched by his verses, not strictly obituary, on the gallstones which afflicted his friend, the incumbent of the Roxbury Parish Church:

> For if thou shoulst be Stoned to death
> And that way pelted out of breath
> Thou wilt like Stephen fall asleep
> And free from pain forever keep.

Upon the death of John Foster, printer, the Reverend Mr. Capen of Topsfield drew the appropriate hope:

> Thy body, which no activeness did lack,
> Now's laid aside, like an old almanack;
> But for the present only's out of date:
> 'Twill have at length a far more active state:

15

NEW ENGLAND SAINTS

Yes, though with dust thy body soiled be,
Yet at the resurrection we shall see
A fair edition, and of matchless worth
Free from erratas, new in heaven set forth;
'Tis but a word from God the great Creator,
It shall be done when He saith, *Imprimatur*.

Perhaps the most elaborate of these witty (but not
frivolous) elegies is "The Grammarian's Funeral" — a
work surely unfamiliar to Browning — composed by Benjamin Tompson, the "Renowned Poet of New England,"
and dispensed in handsome broadside, upon the death of
the venerable and famous Ezekiel Cheever, who, as his
pupil Cotton Mather says, "held the rod for 70 years"
in New England. In this ingenious work the mourners
are not towns, rivers, saints, or poets but the eight parts
of speech: the old schoolmaster's companions and serv-
ants, now summoned to his funeral:

The Clouds of Tears did overcast their faces,
Yea all were in most lamentable *Cases*,
We five *Declensions* did the Work decline,
And told the *Pronoun Tu*, the Work is thine:
But in this case those have no call to go
That want the *Vocative*, and can't say O! . . .
Great honour was confer'd on *Conjugations*,
They were to follow next to the *Relations*.
Amo did love him best, and *Doceo* might
Allege he was his Glory and Delight.
But *Lego* said By me he got his skill,
And therefore next the *Herse* I follow will . . .
A doleful day for *verbs*, they look so *moody*
They drove Spectators to a Mournful Study . . .

Tompson, who was graduated from Harvard in 1662,
sometimes manages a modest conceit:

16

THE PURITAN POETS

His words were Oracles; his fervent Prayers
Like mighty Angels climd the Heavnly stairs,
Battred Heavns Frontiers, entered and came back
With all the blessings which the Church did lack . . .

The Vesper of his life's a constant Cry,
When will deaths curious claws these knots untie?
A crazie cage of bones curtaind with Skin,
A ruind Castle where great strength had beene.

The Reverend Urian Oakes, though born in England, came to the Bay State Colony as a young child, was graduated from Harvard in 1649, and served as President of the College from 1675 to 1681. Increase Mather wrote of him: "It may be said . . . that he was one of the greatest lights that ever shone in this part of the world, or that is ever like to arise in our horizon"; and his son, Cotton, thinks that "America never had a greater master of true, pure, Ciceronian Latin," and canonizes him as "the Lactantius of New England."

Oakes's dearest friend was the Reverend Thomas Shepard of Charlestown, son of the saintly first Pastor of Cambridge. At Harvard's 1678 commencement, President Oakes, in the course of his Latin oration, devoted a long paragraph of panegyric to his recently deceased friend. He also wrote a verse elegy running to fifty-two stanzas, beginning:

Oh! that I were a Poet now in grain!
How would I invocate the Muses all
To deign their presence, lend their flowing Vein,
And help to grace dear *Shepard*'s Funeral!
How would I paint our griefs, and succours borrow
From Art and Fancy, to limn out our sorrow!

President Oakes's elegy is currently praised, and deserves

praise, for its accomplished versification. There was probably no Boston poet so suave as he till the Reverend Mather Byles. Nor can one doubt the tender sincerity of the poem.

But one has moved from the Puritan Baroque into the style of the Restoration. And there is loss as well as gain. Gone are the anagrams, the acrostics, the pious puns. Throughout the fifty-two stanzas, Oakes rigorously avoids the holy play on Shepard, the convergence of name and nature. One turns back regretfully to the Latin elegy composed for the elder Shepard by his friend, the Reverend Peter Bulkly, first minister of Concord, from which Cotton Mather has preserved the lines:

> *Nominis, officiiq; fuit concordia dulcis*
> *Officio pastor, nomine pastor erat.*
> (His name and office sweetly did agree,
> Shepard by name and in his ministry.)

The old Watertown graveyard preserves the Reverend Joshua Moody's Baroque epitaph for Lydia Bailey — not "conscious free verse," as it has been called, but rude (and good) use of assonance and consonance:

Good betimes	Best at last
Lived by faith	Died in grace
Went off singing	Left us weeping.

Not all the elegies and epitaphs were composed by a clergyman or a village poet for solitary use. As late as 1880, the anonymous, almost typical, Puritan epitaph (slightly altered, like the folk ballads) appears on a gravestone in Ogunquit, State of Maine:

> Remember me as you pass by
> As you are now, so once was I

THE PURITAN POETS

And as I am now soon you must be
Prepare for death and follow me.

Like the ancient Greek epitaphs, in the *Greek Anthology*
and elsewhere, the dead man utters his *memento mori*
to the living; and the very unspecificity — in contrast
to the elegies and grandiose monuments which, whether
in Westminster Abbey or a Country Churchyard, celebrate the once celebrated but now forgotten — re-
nounces the precarious standards of this world and absorbs the man on whose slate it is engraved into the
human multitude awaiting God's estimate on Judgment
Day.

As with their contemporaries in old England, the
Romantic sense of 'the poet' was sensibly missing: poets
in prose like the Reverend Robert Burton, Sir Thomas
Browne, Bishop Taylor, and Bishop Ken felt no em-
barrassment at writing verses far less 'poetic' than their
prose. So with the Yankees of the seventeenth century.
Poetry was verse; and one of the obvious reasons for
rhymed verse was its mnemonic character. So children
learned at once their alphabets, theology, and Bible
history from the *New England Primer,* issued prior to
1690 and an American 'best seller':

"In Adam's fall / We sinned all"

down to

"Zachaeus he / Did climb a tree / Our Lord to see."

Somewhat different was the case with another com-
munal versification, the *Bay Psalm Book* (1640). The
Anglicans had no such hymns as those of Dr. Watts and
the Wesleys till the eighteenth century, but, like the
Puritans, sang metrical Psalms, as the Church of Scot-

land does to this day. In 1561, William Kethe brought out a Genevan Psalter in English, containing eighty-seven psalms; in the following year, Sternhold and Hopkins produced a complete Psalter, now termed the 'Old Version.' Archbishop Parker published a version in 1567 with some of the Psalms set by Thomas Tallis; and George Sandys (who made a brief stay in America) did the same, with the accompaniment of twenty-two new tunes by Milton's friend, Henry Lawes. In 1696 came Tate and Brady's 'New Version,' for the most part in the ballad meter later called "C.M." (common measure).

None of these versions, however, satisfied the Massachusetts Bay Colony of emigrants; and, ten years after their landing, Weld, John Eliot, and the first of the Mathers produced the *Bay Psalm Book*.

The important point for all was that the Psalms were directly inspired by God, not of human composition; and the Massachusetts men naturally held that the most rigid rendering of the holy hymns should be made, at whatever distortion of meter and word order. In the original draft of the Preface, the Reverend Richard Mather is explicit in stating the new translators' principles: "Neither let any think, that for the meetre sake wee have taken liberty or poeticall licence to depart from the true and proper sence of Davids [i.e., God's] words in the hebrew verses, noe; but it hath beene one part of our religious care and faithfull endeavour to keepe close to the original text . . . [For] it is not unknowne to the godly learned that they [other translators] have rather presented a paraphrase then the words of David . . . and that their additions to the words, detractions from the words, are not seldome and rare, but very frequent and many times needles . . ."

THE PURITAN POETS

The *Bay Psalm Book* follows the King James translation (as well as the 'Hebrew') closely. But in order to translate God's word — and to manage, after a fashion, meter (the old fourteener) as well as rhyme, something had to be abandoned; and that something is anything approximating the normal English word order of the period. Any syntactical contortion is warranted by closeness to the Word.

The Twenty-third Psalm (which can be sung to the tune of 'Old Eighty-first,' in Day's Psalter of 1562) assumed this form in 1640:

> The Lord to mee a shepheard is, want therefore shall
> not I.
> Hee in the folds of tender-grasse, doth cause mee down
> to lie . . .
> Goodness and mercy surely shall all my dayes follow
> mee:
> And in the Lords house I shall dwell so long as dayes
> shall bee.

Ten years later, President Dunster and Mr. Lyon revised the Psalm Book, "having," they avowed, "a special ey both to the gravity of the phrase" and the "sweetnes of the verse." The attempt at "sweetness" must have aimed at something stylistically smoother; but their version of the same Psalm, when it does not merely reproduce that of their precursors, deteriorates any earlier metrical "sweetness," as one can see from the last couplet of the 'Revised Version':

> Goodness and mercy my dayes all shall surely follow
> me:
> And in the Lords house dwell I shall so long as dayes
> shall bee.

NEW ENGLAND SAINTS

Literality and "sweetness" are not brethren which dwell together in unity. For Anglicans, it was sufficient to translate the substance of a Psalm into the poetic style of the period. Judged by such a theory, Addison wrote an admirable 'metrical psalm,' "The Lord my pasture shall prepare," with a dulcet second stanza offering a "verdant landscape"; and in the nineteenth century, the Reverend Sir H. W. Baker made a version, doubtless not recognized as a 'metrical psalm' but only as a 'favorite hymn': "The King of love my Shepherd is." This High Anglican priest, without neglecting the "rod and the staff," adds a "Cross"; the "table" prepared "before me" becomes an Altar; and the "cup which runneth over" emerges as the Eucharistic "chalice."

Yet these smoother (and looser) versions do not supplant the Church of Scotland's *Psalms of David in Metre* . . . or the *Bay Psalm Book,* books today damned on a literary theory which cannot be accepted as universal. The current theory that poetry must, at least in word order, concur with that of prose is only current theory; and, even at that, the canonization of Father Hopkins' poems ought to give pause. Dislocation (as well as ellipsis; as well as the currently outmoded inversion) is, like alliterative verse or accentual verse, simply a style to be learned, a taste to be acquired.

The Puritan poetry of seventeenth-century New England (dominantly Baroque) is not to be dismissed by Neoclassical standards — whether those of President Oakes or the Reverend Mather Byles, who had the honor of a correspondence with Alexander Pope.

●

ORTHODOX PARSONS OF
CHRIST'S CHURCH

In 1857 and 1859, the Reverend William B. Sprague of Albany published two volumes, *Annals of the American Pulpit* . . . , devoted to "distinguished clergymen" of the "Trinitarian Congregational" faith, subsequently following them with volumes commemorating the Unitarian and Episcopal clergy.

The first two volumes (which celebrate the Puritans, Covenant Calvinists, and Edwardeans of New England's first two centuries) have no real parallel: if one were to be offered, it would be rather Boswell's *Johnson* — or Aubrey's *Lives* — than Walton's golden legends of the Anglican saints; for the *Annals* are composed chiefly of anecdotal letters, and the persons commemorated are, almost without exception, what New England calls 'characters.'

Harriet Beecher Stowe — who was the daughter of

the Reverend Lyman Beecher of Litchfield and later Boston, the sister of the Reverend Henry Ward Beecher of Brooklyn's Plymouth Church, and the wife of a learned professor at Andover Theological School (founded to combat Harvard's Unitarianism), and whose New England novels, notably *Oldtown Folk* and *The Minister's Wooing*, are the best re-creations of theocracy's last days — rightly stressed, in her review of Sprague published in the *Atlantic* for February, 1858, the "racy individuality" of the New England parsons, especially those settled over country parishes.

Sprague limits himself to facts and bibliographies of his divines. The delight of his volumes lies in their "testimony concerning character." For the subjects who died before 1770, direct testimony was not available, and Sprague had resort to 'funeral sermons' and the like and to Cotton Mather's masterpiece, the *Magnalia* — this despite Sprague's objection (which I am far from sharing) to Mather's Baroque style.

After 1770, the formula is almost this: one or more long Augustan letters, written by an octogenarian, recall the writer's childhood memories of the octogenarian under whom, impressed, he 'sat.' Perhaps the most delectable of the 'contributions' to Sprague is the account of Dr. Osgood of Medford, comprising a long and elegant letter from the Doctor's learned daughter, Miss Lucy, and one of equal length and richness from Professor Francis of Harvard, 'catechized' as a child by the Doctor.

Generally delectable is the continuity of the biographies — not the 'apostolic succession' of Anglicans, but an Aaronic continuity of priests, sons and grandsons of priests. There was also the continuity of theological teacher and disciple.

In the Preface to his 1856 edition, Dr. Sprague conveys this 'succession': "Of about 540 individuals who have contributed to this work, 79 are known to be deceased, and 52 *have a place in it both as contributors and subjects.* Quite a number of the contributors have been between 80 and 90 years of age; six between 90 and 100; and one has actually completed his century."

Like Dr. Sprague, I intend not theological history but hagiography; and like him I shall chiefly limn the portraits and recount the 'sayings' of the divines whose spiritual father was the neo-Calvinist Reverend Jonathan Edwards.

'President' Edwards, who lies buried in the old graveyard at Princeton College — where, shortly after his election to that office, he died — was the conscious and unconscious founder of a revival of evangelical religion called the Great Awakening (which aroused in him painfully mixed emotions), and of a theological defiance of 'Pope' Solomon Stoddard — his grandfather, who had brought him to the Church of Christ at Northampton as his 'junior colleague' — and of the Reverend Dr. Chauncy of the First Church of Boston.

Jonathan Edwards was a close theologian; a preacher; a student at first hand of the 'varieties of religious experience'; and the author of *A Treatise Concerning Religious Affections.* He was, I think, one of our few American saints, and a saint of the order of Aquinas; not, like Father Taylor and 'Johnny Appleseed' (Jonathan Chapman), a Protestant 'Franciscan,' but a philosopher, ascetic, and mystic. He married another mystic (Sarah Pierrepont); and among his children he begot another theologian, a second 'President Edwards' — Jonathan Edwards the Younger — of Union College, Schenectady.

But Edwards begot intellectual sons as well as sons

of both loins and mind. In his day, theological schools did not exist (any more than in England); and those who felt a vocation to the ministry were — like young candidates for the bar or the medical profession — trained, and ordinarily boarded, in the parsonage of a clergyman regionally recognized as a systematic theologian and not merely a preacher and parish pastor.

Edwards' parsonage early became such a 'seminary'; and such was his power that New England Congregationalism was split, within his lifetime, into the Old Calvinists and the Edwardeans.

Of Edwards' disciples, many in turn became theologians, making, as they were called, "improvements" on Edwards' theology: the term used was not patronizing or pejorative; it was rather analogous to Newman's 'development of doctrine.' The two chief disciples, Dr. Bellamy of Bethlehem, Connecticut, and Dr. Samuel Hopkins of Newport, Rhode Island, each founded a 'school' or 'line' of neo-Calvinists. Dr. Hopkins, indeed, though physically frail, the pastor of a small parish composed chiefly of elderly women, a great theologian but not an 'organizer,' unwittingly provided his name to a zealous faction in the New England Church — the 'Hopkinsians.'

In contrast to the Old Calvinists (out of whom, almost concurrently, there developed, primarily in Boston, Salem, Hingham — that is, within the immediate territory of Harvard College — the rationalists later to be called Unitarian), the Edwardeans, primarily centered in the Connecticut River Valley, were attached, as their founder was, to Yale and were commonly country parsons. A remarkable group of men, they did not seek, or accept, 'preferment.'

After college and study with some orthodox minister,

they were wont to be called by a parish — in those days in effect an 'established church,' one to a village. Sometimes they had a 'glebe' to till, and, farm-reared, gladly tilled; sometimes, like Dr. Emmons, they refused to surrender any time from their books. Celibacy was almost as rare among them as among the parish priests of the Greek Church: seemed indeed abnormal. But wife — or successive wives — and children were kept in their place, as they were by Moses and Aaron. Current habits of turning the Protestant Church into a social center of geniality or *'going about* doing good' were neither obligatory nor customary. The absence of 'pastoral calls' was not resented — the call, that is, which is not a *religious call.*

Once settled over a parish, the clergyman commonly stayed for life, commonly a very long life. To be ordained at twenty and stay till eighty would almost be the norm. He came, according to the then system, as junior colleague to an octogenarian (as Edwards' career had begun) and ended his pastorate with, in turn, the aid of a junior colleague.

The great Dr. Emmons, minister for his lifetime to Franklin, Massachusetts, retired from his pastorate at eighty-five. He chose his own successor, a proper Edwardean; and at the public installation of the new pastor, he gave to the Reverend Mr. Smalley the solemn 'charge': "I feel . . . as Aaron felt when Moses, at the divine command, took him, and Eleazar his son, up to Mount Hor . . . ; and there stripped off his sacerdotal robes, and put them upon Eleazar his son and successor in the most holy and sacred office on earth."

Some 'weak brothers' there were, of course, whom parishes had to get rid of; but they were infrequent. In a real sense, the 'theocracy' lingered on till, say, the

27

death of Emerson's stepgrandfather, the Reverend Ezra Ripley, ordained minister of Concord, 1778; died, 1841; characterized by Emerson in a brilliant and delicious memoir written just after its subject's death.

The long pastorate had an impressive effect: the same pastor baptized, married, buried as many as three generations of a family. Nor was he free, like a 'revivalist,' to give a series of striking and 'soul-stirring' sermons and then move on to repeat the same. And his life, ever open to the inspection of his village neighbors, was a constant witness.

He was an educator as well as a shepherd of the flock. The days of the long pastorate were also the days of the long sermon, extending to a couple of hours in the morning, followed (after a cold lunch eaten in the Sabbath House) by another discourse. These sermons of the Edwardean 'line' were rarely emotional: they were sequentially written and closely reasoned, so that — as innumerable testimonies witness — eighteenth-century New Englanders, like their contemporaries in Scotland, received a liberal education from arguing the pastor's argument all the week.

The Reverend Convers Francis — Transcendentalist, and Professor at Harvard — says of Dr. Osgood, pastor of Medford: "When I was a youth, the Doctor commenced a series of expositions of the Old Testament as a part of his pulpit services . . . They were listened to with great interest, for the most part, and were so written as to be instructive and edifying, even to the least enlightened part of the congregation. Though they contained a considerable share of learned criticism I remember that my father, a mechanic, and with but a slender education, was always delighted with them and used to talk about them after meeting, as indeed he did about the preaching generally . . . "

Yet this serious and sequential discourse was commonly united with simplicity, even rusticity, of speech — appropriate alike to preacher and congregation. The clergy commonly wrote, and read, their sermons, though usually making a point to memorize the 'affective' passages of their discourses. Francis remembered from his childhood that at such passages Dr. Osgood would deliberately take off his spectacles: then "We always knew that something good and great was coming . . . "

The long pastorate and the single church (the *parish* church) gave power to the parson, often the dominant figure in the village. Often, like Anglican vicars in England, he was eccentric — often outspoken as he would not have allowed others to be; oftener than not, he was possessed of a sharply witty tongue; sometimes richly grotesque in his humor. All this was tolerated by the parish: like the university don, and the vicar, he was not expected — for good or ill — to be like ordinary people; and the authority of the Church gave its incumbent something approaching both judicial and sacerdotal power. In a real sense he had 'the power of the keys.'

Most of these eighteenth-century pastors (called 'Father' as they grew old) were settled over rural parishes. They could not afford large libraries like Cotton Mather's 2,000. The great Edwards owned but 500 books; his son, 250. But that did not disturb men accustomed, from their college days, to keeping — like seventeenth-century students at Oxford and Cambridge — 'commonplace' books into which they copied passages (often indexed) from books borrowed from university libraries or from their friends.

NEW ENGLAND SAINTS

Jonathan Fisher (1768–1847, minister of the isolated and ill-paying parish of Blue Mill, Maine) kept 'commonplace' books daily, devising his own shorthand code when he was a Harvard student in 1792. He was also an author, painter, and linguist. In his college days he made water-color paintings of birds and animals; he painted in oils, which he mixed himself; when he published *Scripture Animals . . . Written Especially for the Young*, he illustrated it with woodcut engravings of his own.

Fisher made his own Hebrew lexicon, which preceded the learned work of Gesenius; a friend saw him pore over an Arabic New Testament unaided by either grammar or lexicon. At family devotions, he was accustomed to read aloud from the divine languages, Hebrew and Greek.

These Congregational parsons limited neither their reading nor their 'commonplace' books to the Protestant Fathers. Fisher's extracts included St. Augustine and à Kempis; and, strangest, Pascal appears in his Journals for fifty years. Emmons had the special good fortune of having housed in his parsonage both the Town Library (given by Benjamin Franklin, after whom the town was named) and the Parish Library. Into his 'commonplace' book he put long quotations and abstracts not only from those of his own persuasion but from the great Anglican divines — among them, Hooker, author of the *Ecclesiastical Polity*, Bishop Bull, and Dr. Waterland, and from the saintly Catholic Archbishop, Fénelon. But, like the other scholar-parsons, Emmons did not limit himself to theology: an early 'commonplace' book of his contains notes on chronology, history, geography, and psychology.

The parson's reading was not, however, like that of

nineteenth-century preachers, for display — that the Sunday discourse might be 'literary' in style and adorned with excerpts from "the poets." He read to think and to discipline others to thinking. When Emerson marveled at the *Sitzfleisch* of the nineteenth-century German scholars, with their twelve, fourteen, sixteen hours of work, he was obviously not aware that New England had once produced the like. "We read," says Dr. Park, epigone of the Edwardeans, "of the two Edwards, Hopkins, Smalley, Stiles, Chauncy, and Dwight at their books thirteen, fourteen, fifteen, and sometimes eighteen hours a day."

These men were not 'covering ground'; they were 'close readers.' Here are some of Dr. Emmon's maxims, addressed primarily, of course, to himself: "Read with a particular object in view." "Never despair of a student who has *one clear idea.*" "He is a learned man who understands one subject, and a very learned man who understands two." And finally, "I believe there is scarcely any circumstance which has a more direct tendency to turn *learned men into sceptics* than *reading too much* and *thinking too little.*"

When Andover Seminary was being founded, some of his admirers wanted Emmons to become its chief Professor of Theology; but Emmons said he preferred to remain a preacher to farmers — a harder thing; for, as the great Anglican Archbishop of Ireland, Dr. Ussher, was wont to say, "It requires all our learning to make things plain."

Emmons had his reward. Instead of seeking preferment to Andover or Boston, he educated and saved Franklin, Massachusetts.

Grandiosely, John Wesley said "The *world* is my parish." Said Emmons, "Franklin must be the *center of my world;* and my study must be the center of Franklin." In consequence, when a stranger inquired, in nearby towns, for the road to Franklin, he was told, "*That road* will take you to Dr. Emmons." Both Wesley's maxim and Emmons' will lead one to power; but I fancy that, as a Kantian axiom, "Act so that the maxim of thy will can be at the same time accepted as the principle of a universal legislation," Emmons' maxim is the sounder. "Teach me, my God and King, in all towns, Thee to see."

In reviewing the *Annals* for the *Atlantic,* Mrs. Stowe remarks, "A collection of the table-talk of the clergy whose lives are sketched in Dr. Sprague's volumes would be a rare fund of humor, shrewdness, genius, and originality"; and, remembering the parsonage at Litchfield in which she, so eager a combination of theologian and storyteller, was reared, she cavils that the "written record" in the *Annals* "falls far below that traditional one which floated about us [Beechers] in our earlier years."

What Mrs. Stowe misses is, I make out, in large part the reproduction of New England theology, in all its possible metaphysicality, spoken in New England dialect. Here she is not wholly just to Sprague's correspondents, or to the 468-page *Memoir of Emmons . . .* (1861) which was to follow in three years; but assuredly no one had Mrs. Stowe's rich sense of doctrine, dialect, and 'characters.'

She gives a specimen of what she could do in "Old Father Morris," drawn from the life and sermons of the Reverend Samuel John Mills, Pastor of Torrington, in Litchfield County, Connecticut. Unlike the two excellent epistolary biographers of Mills in Sprague, Mrs.

Stowe reproduces his speech in "the strong provinciality of Yankee dialect."

She remembers his sermons, preached from her father's pulpit in Litchfield, and how, in his hands, the Gospels, particularly dear to him, "became a gallery of New England paintings." He described the walk to Emmaus: the road is "a New England turnpike; you can see its milestones, its mullein stalks, its toll gates . . . Emmaus rises in the distance, in the likeness of a New England village, with a white meeting-house and spire."

At Jerusalem, Jesus "used to get tired of the noise" and get "tired of preaching, again and again, to people who would not mind a word he said . . . " What a relief to visit the house of Mary and Martha: "A little white house among the trees; you could just see it from Jerusalem." It was restful even though Martha was busy around the house "frying fritters and making gingerbread."

And there was Father Mills, preaching on the text, "The High and Holy One that inhabiteth eternity." He told the people of Litchfield about the Great God — the Great Jehovah — and then about the people of this world, how they were "flustering and worrying, and afraid they should not get time to do this, and that, and t'other. *But the Lord's never in a hurry; he has it all to do, but he has time enough, — for he inhabiteth eternity.*"

People remembered the "odd sayings" of Dr. Bellamy who, when someone had built a fire of green wood, said, as might have said Emily of Amherst, "Warm me here! I'd as soon try to warm me by starlight on the north side of a tombstone!" — this from the great theologian, Dr. Bellamy, whose *True Religion Delineated and Distin-*

guished from All Counterfeits was prefatorily commended by the Reverend Jonathan Edwards; and they remembered Dr. Azel Backus, "another of those wilder and more erratic temperaments" — Dr. Backus who occasionally indulged himself in ludicrous comparisons — who rarely delivered a sermon without weeping and not infrequently melted his whole congregation in tears.

The neo-Calvinists: these were great men — powerful among their fellows as the representatives of the Divine Sovereignty, humble and self-abnegatory in the presence of the Infinite Omnipotent. Both God and man cannot be free. Our *merits* cannot win us *Grace;* "None is holy but God," and this holiness is not to be anthropomorphically conceived. Edwards' two disciples, Drs. Emmons and Hopkins, remained to the end uncertain of their salvation.

Like the French Quietists, these men taught the exacting doctrine that our business is to *love God,* not to assure ourselves of His love for us. In Dr. Hopkins' maxim, the test of a true Christian is his willingness to be damned for the Glory of God, one's *"disinterested benevolence."*

Those are strong — as these men were — who trust everything, even their own salvation, not to human righteousness but to the judgment of Him Who alone is King and Ruler, waiting, in despair or in hope, for that Day when God shall be *all in all.*

NEO-PLATONIC ALCOTT

Bronson Alcott — probably the most representative, certainly the most picturesque figure among the New England Transcendentalists — does not deserve to reach posterity as the impractical parent of a storyteller for girls. Though a butt for the satire of the Philistine among his contemporaries, he won and held the respect of the intellectuals of his day both as man and as thinker.

His idiom of thought was archaic: Alcott was "a neo-Platonist born at the wrong time, belatedly or prematurely incarnate, a sort of survival"; but his "universe of discourse" was genuine, not histrionic. Among the Transcendentalists moved this mystic and sage, extracting his dole of individualistic indulgence quite as much in retrospective as in anticipatory gaze. He accepted his post in the world: the time, the place, the circumstances were God-appointed.

By profession, Alcott was a sage; by trade, a pedagogue. He conducted experimental and 'advanced' schools in Cheshire, Connecticut, Philadelphia, and Boston; actually superintended the public schools of sacred Concord for a few years; and, in extreme old age, gratified lifelong ambitions in the founding and maintenance of the Concord Summer School of Philosophy, a notable venture into the metaphysical empyrean.

For nearly fifty years Alcott practiced the Transcendentalist calling in 'conversation,' which served him as vehicle of expression as the lecture served Emerson. He led, as his neighbor wrote, "the life of a peripatetic philosopher, conversing in cities and villages wherever invited, on divinity, on human nature, on ethics, on dietetics, and a wide range of practical questions."

As a missionary from Transcendentalist New England, he journeyed as far west as St. Louis, where he had the good fortune to encounter an eager set of Hegelians, one of whom, W. T. Harris, became his most intelligent interpreter. Everywhere he 'conversed,' his presence gathered the speculative minds — the young, in a state of *Aufklärung;* the old, persistent in a mood of inquiry.

Alcott's own intellectual development may be traced with considerable definiteness from 1825 on, when, with his uncle Dr. Bronson (then at the head of the Cheshire Academy), he was reading books like Dwight's theology, Stewart and Locke on the philosophy of the mind, and Watts's logic — in short, standard eighteenth-century discipline for the 'understanding.'

The turn of thought commonly denominated Transcendental appears in his diary as early as 1826, and appears quite without derivation: "Where [he asks] is the individual who boldly dares assert opinions differing with pre-established notions — dares to think for himself? ... And millions of minds are in this state of slavery to authority of books and dogmas and tyranny. How shall they escape? Rebel. Think for themselves; let others grumble. Dare to be singular; let others deride."

In 1827, he attacks the doctrines of the Incarnation and the Trinity — attacks for which, fourteen years later, Theodore Parker was excommunicated by the Unitarians of Dr. Channing's school: "Those who at the present day idolise the person of Jesus Christ, asserting him to be God, exhibit the disposition of men in ancient times to deify such of their fellow-men as performed great and magnanimous actions ... Jesus unquestionably was a great and good man, a prodigy of the time in which he lived ... His was the best system of ethics which had been offered to man; it was adapted to his situation and wants at the time. But I am not sure that in all respects it is equally adapted to the present state. I am unwilling to admit that while improvement in every other science is striding forward with rapidity, nothing is to be effected in the all-concerning science of religion."

Reared in tenets and practices of the Episcopal Church, about the time of these entries Alcott ceased to think of himself as an Anglican, dissenting from liturgy as well as dogma. Of the Book of Common Prayer, he wrote: "Nothing natural, original, or spontaneous was permitted to appear. The primitive, beaten path track of former generations is thought the only right way among this people, who forget that modes and systems should often be changed to suit the changes of improving society, and that the Spirit alone is essential."

37

During his operation of private schools in Philadelphia from 1831 to 1834, Mr. Alcott had access to a number of rich libraries; and his serious reading, especially in philosophy, had here its inception. He made himself familiar with Plato and Aristotle and Bacon, with Coleridge and Carlyle and Shelley. It was Coleridge, he later testified, who introduced him to metaphysical idealism:

"In 1833 I was a disciple of Experience, trying to bring my theories within the Baconian method of Induction and took the philosophy of Aristotle as the exponent of humanity, while my heart was even then lingering around the theories of Plato, without being conscious of it. A follower of Aristotle was I in theory, yet a true Platonist in practice. Christianity had not found its philosophical interpretation at that time in my heart; its spirit was striving for forms agreeable to the understanding. The heart's problems were seeking solution from the skill of the head. I was looking outward for the origin of the human powers, making more of phenomena than I ought; studying the concrete, without a sense of the grounds on which this was dependent for its form and continuance. It was Coleridge that lifted me out of this difficulty. The perusal of the *Aids to Reflection*, the *Friend*, and the *Biographia Literaria* at this time gave my mind a turn toward the spiritual. I was led deeper to seek the grounds even of experience, and found the elements of human consciousness not in impressions of external nature, but in the spontaneous life of the Spirit itself, independent of experience in space and time. Thus was I relieved from the philosophy of sense."

This estimate of Coleridge did not lapse. In 1872, S. T. C. still seemed "the most stimulating of modern British thinkers. He had wider sympathies with pure thought, and cast more piercing glances into its essence and laws than any contemporary."

The twelfth chapter of *Biographia Literaria,* with its citations from Plotinus, may well have introduced Alcott to that historic school of thought with which he was in congenital harmony, neo-Platonism. It would appear to be from Coleridge that he derived the notion of a "union of the Christian with the Platonic" philosophy, which he registers, in 1833, as his aim in common with Dr. Channing.

From 1834, Alcott superintended his celebrated Temple School, Boston's venture in 'progressive' education, the chronicles of which remain fare for thought as well as for wonder; continued his reading in philosophy; and began to teach the Platonic doctrine of the pre-existence and subsequent lapse of the soul.

In 1835 he made the acquaintance of Concord's chief citizen. Emerson has been charged with inordinate admiration for his friend; and of course his was certainly "a faith approaching to superstition concerning admirable persons . . . " But Emerson surely erred less than Alcott's Philistine detractors, for with his balance of poetry and prudence, with his "Greek head on right Yankee shoulders," he was in a position to comprehend Alcott's real virtues, yet to preserve the proper refusal of complete capitulation.

Without denying Carlyle's view that Alcott was a sort of contemporary Don Quixote, Emerson added that his audience always played Sancho Panza. Emerson found the knight-errant venerable rather than absurd — a wanderer from another world, to be sure, a little dazed and inarticulate, but none the less luminous. An obscure neo-Platonist, Thomas Johnson, mystically addressed Mr. Alcott as "one of the brightest of 'Heaven's exiles straying from the orb of light.' " Though not a sharer in the cosmology of the 'lapse,' Emerson rendered, on empirical grounds, a similar verdict. "Our Alcott [he wrote] has only just missed being a seraph. A little English finish and articulation to his potentialities, and he would have compared with the greatest . . . "Alcott came, the magnificent dreamer, brooding, as ever, on the renewal or re-edification of the social fabric after ideal law, heedless that he has been uniformly rejected by every class to whom he has addressed himself, and just as sanguine and vast as ever . . . Very pathetic it is to see this wandering Emperor from year to year making his round of visits from house to house of such as do not exclude him, seeking a companion, tired of pupils."

A contemporary Don Quixote, a strayed seraph, an exiled heir to the throne, an itinerant emperor: Emerson will add yet one more analogy:

"Alcott is a simple person, a natural Levite, a priest forever after the order of Melchizedek, whom all good persons readily combine, one would say, to maintain as a priest by voluntary contribution to live in his own cottage, literary and spiritual, and choosing his own methods of teaching and action."

Unanalogically, Emerson declared his friend "the most refined and advanced soul we have had in New England, who makes all other souls appear slow and cheap and mechanical; a man of such courtesy and greatness, that (in conversation) all others, even the intellectual, seem sharp and fighting for victory, and angry . . ."

This estimate was not the aberration of a first ardor. Emerson's son testifies that his father, "through the long years of their acquaintance, always said that he found more stimulus and elevation in private talk with Mr. Alcott than with any other man." And the last considered notice of Alcott in the *Journals* (August 1866) yields in pitch to none preceding:

"As pure intellect, I have never seen his equal. The people with whom he talks do not even understand him. They interrupt him with clamorous dissent, or what they think verbal endorsement of what they fancy he may have been saying . . . ; and do not know that they have interrupted his large and progressive statement, do not know that all they have in their baby brains is spotty and incoherent, that all he sees and says is like astronomy, lying there real and vast, and every part and fact in eternal connection with the whole . . . Alcott's activity of mind is shown in the perpetual invention and felicity of his language . . . The moral benefits of such a mind cannot be told. The world fades: men, reputations, politics, shrivel: the interests, powers, futures of the soul beam a new dayspring. Faith becomes sight."

Though always, to himself, John the Baptist, ever in search of the Messiah to come, Emerson was no fool in his judgment of men, even when they were 'idealists.' His 'compensations' for his faith are not to be doubted.

Alcott, in short, must not be set down as a half-pathetic, half-boring, pensioner of his illustrious friend. The idealistic philosophy reached Emerson through a variety of minds: through Cudworth and Berkeley and Swedenborg and Plato and the Oriental scriptures. But these were voices from the library; and books were to Emerson confirmations rather than sources. The intuitions in his own spirit were primary; and he found in Alcott a contemporary and neighbor who affirmed with a firmer assurance than Emerson could command this primacy of the spirit. The "Orphic poet" in the concluding chapter of *Nature* is Alcott. "I shall write on his tomb," said Emerson, "there lies Plato's reader":

"It were too much to say [Emerson wrote in his *Journals*] that the Platonic world I might have learned to treat as cloudland, had I not known Alcott, who is a native of that country, yet I will say that he makes it as solid as Massachusetts to me . . ."

His Platonism was not, however, primarily reproductory: he was *anima naturaliter Platonica*. To call him a Platonist would be wrongly to attribute "secondariness to the highly original habit of his salient and intuitive mind." A reader of Plato, the neo-Platonists, and 'the mystics,' Alcott taught doctrines akin to theirs not from erudition but from perception.

It was another, and blessed, virtue of Alcott's that he could listen as well as expound: and Emerson needed a listener. Emerson found in Alcott a spirit hospitable to all conceivable ideas and ideals, save only those of the market place:

"Alcott [he writes in his *Journals*] is a certain fluid in which men of a certain spirit can easily expand themselves and swim at large, they who elsewhere found themselves confined . . . Me has he served now these twelve years in that way; he was the reasonable creature to speak to that I wanted."

To be sure, Alcott was limited in his themes of discourse. Life found interpretation through two or three persistent doctrines; one was always being brought back to the temperaments, or the lapse, or the One. In his *Journals*, Emerson writes:

"They say of Alcott, and I have sometimes assented, that he is one-toned, and hearkens with no interest to books or conversations out of the scope of his one commanding idea. May be so, but very different is his centralism from that of vulgar monomaniacs . . . "

But what of that? Alcott's habitual themes were of the grandest; his habitual level of thought was of the most elevated. To plenty of others one could talk of cabbages and kings; not so easily was one to obtain converse with an American Pythagoras or Jamblichus or Boehme; and such a persistent affirmer of the primacy of the spirit dwelt within distance of an easy stroll down Emerson's own road.

The Transcendentalist Club began its irregular sessions in 1836; in 1840, the *Dial*, designed as the literary organ of Transcendentalism, was inaugurated with Margaret Fuller and George Ripley as its editors, to be succeeded by Emerson. Mr. Alcott was one of the original members of the Club; and the first instalment of his *Orphic Sayings* appeared in the initial number of the magazine.

The *Sayings* occasioned much silly laughter in the Boston newspapers and the drawing rooms of Beacon Hill. Novel, extravagant, and esoteric, to Bostonians they offered the fitting reduction to the absurd of Transcendentalist cloudland. But the contemporary reader at all versed in the history of philosophy will fancy the laughter in the main unenlightened, certainly not proceeding from any sounder metaphysics.

Alcott's first attempt at a literary exposition of his doctrines, the *Orphic Sayings*, is less systematic than his later versions. His hope that the *Sayings* would comprise a "complete series of sentences, which would carry the appreciative reader through the descent from spirit to matter, and upward again to the first origin" was imperfectly realized. Yet I prefer them over the expanded versions in *Tablets* and *Table-Talk*. Ranging from the aphorism to the *pensée*, they remain definitely within the genre, whatever we name it, which runs from John Burnet's *Early Greek Philosophers* through Pascal to Joubert and beyond. What are offered constitute not reasoned discourses, or treatises proceeding from the understanding: they are intimations, vatic utterances, revelations from the soul to the soul. The seers and sages of India, of Palestine, of Greece, had taught in dark sayings: Alcott, as sage and seer *redivivus*, speaks in similar wise.

In doctrine the *Sayings* combine the teachings of Transcendental individualism as they have become familiar to us through the essays of Emerson with a strain peculiar to Alcott among the Transcendentalists — his neo-Platonism. Emerson was sympathetic to some aspects of the Plotinian teaching, but Emerson was an evolutionist. Alcott was an emanationist; he held to the theory of creation by lapse from the One:

"The soul works from centre to periphery, veiling her labour from the ken of the senses . . . Appearance, though first to sense, is last in the order of generation . . .

"The popular genesis is historical. It is written to sense not to the soul. [According to this fallacious theory] two principles, diverse and alien, interchange the Godhead and sway the world by turns. God is dual. Spirit is derivative . . . Yet in the true genesis, nature is globed in the material, souls orbed in the spiritual firmament. Love globes, wisdom orbs, all things. As magnet the steel, so spirit attracts matter . . . All genesis is love. Wisdom is her form: beauty her costume."

Such the metaphysic of *emanation*. If we translate this descent from spirit through intellect into matter and sense, we discover the history of the soul:

NEO-PLATONIC ALCOTT

"All life is eternal; there is none other; and all unrest is but the struggle of the soul to reassure herself of her inborn immortality; to recover her lost intuition of the same, by reason of her descent amidst the lusts and worship of the idols of flesh and sense . . . The soul's 'vague strivings, and Cyclopean motions confess an aim beyond the confines of transitory natures; she is quivered with heavenly desires: her quarry is above the stars: her arrows are snatched from the armoury of heaven.' "

In his fine elegy upon Emerson, Alcott versifies:

> Come, then, Mnemosyne! and on me wait,
> As if for Ion's harp thou gav'st thine own;
> Recall the memories of man's ancient state,
> Ere to this lost orb had his form dropt down,
> Clothed in the cerements of his chosen fate;
> Oblivious here of heavenly glories flown,
> Lapsed from the high, the fair, the blest estate,
> Unknowing these, and by himself unknown . . .

With Emerson, Alcott deplores reliance upon majorities, institutions, money; and with Emerson, he invokes self-reliance, the religion of the spirit, plain living, and high thinking. But for his ethics Alcott presupposes the metaphysics not of Coleridge but of Plotinus and Proclus. He takes up a tradition which, never totally extinct, is today enjoying a genuine revival among philosophical scholars.

No doubt there were subsidiary elements of the fantastic in the mind of Bronson Alcott, but in the main that mind grasped with clarity and maintained with persistence a world-view ever an option of the philosophically minded.

45

EMERSON, PREACHER TO HIMSELF

To take Emerson as an oracle, or orator, or a systematic philosopher is to mistake him. After the fashion of his Puritan ancestors in England and New England, he is a diarist, the writer of spiritual memoirs and 'spiritual letters.' Whatever comparable rank we assign him, the names with which his belongs are those of Montaigne, Pascal, Amiel, Nietzsche. He is not primarily a 'maker,' either of poetry or philosophy, but a 'seeker.'

Like his approximate contemporaries, Marx and Kierkegaard, Emerson thought that ideas should have consequences. Said Marx: "The philosophers have only interpreted the world in various ways; the point, however, is to change it." Said Kierkegaard: "In the early days of antiquity, the philosopher was a power, moral power, character; the [Roman] empire safeguarded itself by recompensing them, by making them into dons. The don is the eunuch; but he has not emasculated himself for the sake of the Kingdom of Heaven but on the contrary in order to fit better with this characterless world."

A Harvard man, Emerson felt the timidity of the academic mind, saw how the flight from oneself and society might flatteringly name itself detachment, disinterestedness, and objectivity. A New Englander, he found the Boston of his time lacking in conviction and its consequence, force. Upon such an audience, one must enjoin audacity. "It is a sort of maxim with me," he wrote, "never to harp on the omnipotence of limitations. Least of all do we need any suggestion of *checks* and *measures*, as if New England were anything else."

Attacking caution, Emerson addresses first the New England in himself. The great preacher denounces his own obsessive sins; replies, over and over, to his own recurrent scepticisms.

The early *Journals* document Emerson's adolescence. A penetrating self-analyst, he lashed away at himself, lacerated himself. As an undergraduate at Harvard, he was painfully given to desiring this man's art and that man's scope, finding himself inferior in one and another respect, castigating himself for failures and his sloth. At seventeen, he writes of "feeling the humiliating sense of dependence and inferiority, which, like the goading, soul-sickening sense of extreme poverty, palsies efforts." Upon being arrived at the age of nineteen, he takes relentless stock: "I am he who nourished brilliant visions of future grandeur . . ." But he charges himself with being "too tired and too indolent to travel up the mountain path" to glory. As for his heart, he analyzed: "Ungenerous and selfish, cautious and cold, I yet wish to be romantic; [but] have not sufficient feeling to speak a natural hearty welcome to a friend or stranger . . . "

Emerson's famous optimism was not congenital. He was natively introverted, self-conscious, socially embarrassed; without small talk, handy practical skills, the assurance of wealth, or physical presence. In his late essay, "Success," he spoke out of his own casebook when, replying doubtless to older New Englanders, professed believers in the wholesome effect of reproof and censure and 'discipline,' he wrote: "A cynic can chill and dishearten me with a single word. Despondency comes readily enough to the most sanguine . . . " He exhorted to self-reliance and courage and calm because he felt their lack.

The crisis in Emerson's life occurred in his thirtieth year when he resigned his pastorate at the Second Church of Boston. For a frail, cultivated young man without 'means,' such a decision was — to speak prudentially — heroic. Withdrawal from a profession of which the restraints, whether ritual or doctrinal, were so slight, struck some of his clerical colleagues as "Quakerish." There were, says his official biographer, Cabot, "loud whispers of mental derangement." John Quincy Adams notes in his *Journals*: "A son of my once-loved friend William Emerson, and a classmate of my lamented George, after failing in the everyday avocations of a Unitarian preacher and schoolmaster, starts a new doctrine of Transcendentalism . . . "

The particular issue with the Second Church, his scrupulous refusal to celebrate the Lord's Supper, was but specimen and symptom, surely, and so appeared to his sensible contemporaries. Emerson hoped for a professorship of rhetoric at such a college as Bowdoin or Colby or Middlebury; but no chair was offered. What reason to think that, installed, he would not discover some scruple — refuse to employ a textbook, or decline to lecture on mornings when he found he had nothing really to say?

So he passed from being priest with hieratic tenure to being an itinerant prophet. The 'Autocrat' Holmes, who neither understood nor shared Emerson's spirit, is witness that Emerson "accepted a precarious employment, which hardly kept him above poverty, rather than wear the *golden padlock* on his lips which has held fast the conscience of so many pulpit Chrysostoms." Yet this he did without assurance that he had any better equivalent to offer society. Returning from Europe, in 1833, he could not honestly wish away the dominant religion of rural New England. "I see or believe in the wholesomeness of Calvinism for thousands and thousands . . . Ah me! what hope of reform . . . if they who have what they call the light are so selfish and timid and cold, and their faith so impractical and, in their judgment, so unsuitable for the middling classes."

To this scepticism he never found a theoretical answer. The journal entry goes on, however, to his practical decision: "This my charge, plain and clear, to act faithfully upon my own faith; to live by it myself, and see what a hearty obedience to it will do." Not for him the pragmatism of saying what one believed the community needed to hear even though the teacher or preacher couldn't himself privately believe it.

During his preparation for the ministry, and even more persistently during his brief exercise of it, Emerson had sought for the ultimate psychological and moral bases of religion. Authority of persons, even divine persons, must, he concluded, be derivative from some ultimate ground of self-evidence in ethical law or the nature of reality. Earnestly impressed by the psychological and social power which religion had exerted in the past, he believed it must be possible to translate that power into spiritual laws which, not upon authority, a modern man could accept.

One summer, Emerson worked at haying with a Methodist laborer named Tarbox, who, "though ignorant and rude, had some deep thoughts." All men are always praying, he said; and all their prayers are answered. On this theme, Emerson preached his first sermon, in his Uncle Ripley's First Parish Church of Waltham, drawing from his friend's spiritual postulates the warning that we should be careful that we pray for the right things.

Under "prayer," Emerson subsumes the directed action of the will and the imagination, all psychological and moral — as distinguished from physical — force. It is self-definition, recollection, concentration. In his first book, *Nature*, he speaks of "the action of man upon nature with his entire force . . . [of] many obscure . . . facts now arranged under the name of Animal Magnetism, prayer, eloquence, self-healing . . ." In his late *Conduct of Life*, the Waltham sermon recurs, translated into "What we pray to ourselves for is always granted."

During his pastorate at the Second Church of Boston, Emerson filled his *Journals* with meditations on spiritual laws. He developed — or at least repeated, rephrased, and illustrated — what, at twenty-three, he called "my own notions of compensation," attributing the doctrine, if not the word, to Bishop Butler's *Analogy*.

One kind of apologist for religion undertakes to argue the existence of a better world from the manifest chaos and misery of this; but, like the Cambridge Platonists, and Shaftesbury, and Butler, Emerson was not satisfied by such 'argument from defect.' We infer, he believed with them, a future perfect justice from the evidence of justice, however imperfect, operating in this present world.

Under "compensation" Emerson subsumes his whole conception of "spiritual laws" — two distinct ideas each of which has historic claims to the term. The first is that of justice as counterbalance between deformities, or deficiencies, and talents — the psychological law by which a felt inferiority may incite a man to a retrieving triumph. The second is the conception of justice as correspondence between cause and effect, work and wage: it is the Oriental law of Karma; it is the principle enunciated by Jesus the Christ that "whatsoever a man soweth, that shall he also reap."

From the early *Journals* to the late essays, illustrations and applications abound. On counterbalance: "Every defeat in one manner is made up in another. Every suffering is rewarded; — every debt is paid." On correspondence: "The thief steals from himself; — whoso borrows runs into his own debt . . ." "Do you not see that every misfortune is misconduct, that every honor is desert, that every affront is an insolence of your own?"

Of the two motifs Emerson subsumed under "compensation," the deeper is not counterbalance (ultimately the argument from defect, the irrational leap) but correspondence (like begets like). And increasingly important to him is the insistence that 'compensation' is always *in kind*. Like virtue, so learning is its own reward. The 'rewards' of religion, like the 'evidences' adduced in its 'proof,' must themselves be religious. He satirized the "vulgar" doctrine of postmortem rewards and punishments: the orthodox preacher whose sermon implied that

Christians would have, after death, " 'such a good time as the sinners have now'; or, to push it to its extreme import, 'you sin now; we shall sin by and by . . .' " Heaven, as Emerson had read in the Cambridge Platonists, Swedenborg, and *passim* in spiritual writers and mystics (corroborating his own insight), is first a state and only secondarily or correspondentially a place; and we cannot possibly 'go to heaven' unless we already have the kingdom of heaven within us.

In Emerson's latest essays, the spiritual laws of compensation continue to engage him. Means must correspond to ends: "If I strike, I am struck; if I chase, I am pursued." Forms of aggression provoke counterassault, or at least the reaction of resentment. Aggression begets aggression. From this, and other 'vicious circles,' one can make his way out only through self-analysis and reorientation. "What would it avail me if I could *destroy my enemies?* There would be as many to-morrow. That which I hate and fear is really in myself, and no knife is long enough to reach its heart." There is nothing to hate save hate; and nothing to fear save fear. When I can love my enemies, I shall have none, that is, I shall not think of them as enemies.

Between the earlier essays and those in the later volumes ("Fate," "Power," "Success," and "Courage"), there is, however, a shift of proportion, emphasis, tone. Mystical discourses like "The Oversoul" disappear, as do theological terms. The new essays, realistic of outlook and diction, are meditations in 'practical psychology.' In the lineage of "self-reliance," they go back, of course, to Emerson's own experience and the self-explorations carried on in the *Journals;* they restate, simply, what he had learned from his self-therapy. Of James's basic types of religious experience, Emerson is specimen and progenitor of the "once-born," those whose depressions and malaises the 'faith-cure' can dispel. The more severe neurosis of powerful, tormented, divided natures in need of conversion, the 'second birth,' Emerson did not understand from experience; but his empathic grasp of orthodox religion as, in psychological terms, a source of healing and power, gave backing to James's whole treatment of religion as "religious experience."

The doctrine of "compensation" developed early enough so that Emerson learned to bear his frailties tolerantly, supposing them the *defects of his virtues:* for example, his incapacity for intimacy he concedes to be something he cannot remedy and something for which he is recompensed by his gift of public communication, of the public soliloquy which each individual feels addressed to him, *solus ad solum.*

Like Irving Babbitt, Emerson would desire to unite East and West; and, like Babbitt, he would judge the East to have preserved the purer tradition in religion. Emerson's attempt to restate, positively and experimentally, what Western orthodoxy had stated on dogmatic and institutional authority, was to be Babbitt's motive for the homage to Emerson so unexpectedly proffered in the conclusion to the *Masters of Modern French Criticism.* Babbitt's "higher will" is Emerson's "oversoul"; his "higher imagination" Emerson's favorite agency, the creator of ideal images of moral action. The "higher will" is "compensation"; the "higher imagination" is "prayer."

But Babbitt, and Aldous Huxley after him, rightly draw back from Emerson's inability to distinguish between the power of religion as such and the power of spiritual religion. There are religions and religions. As Father Taylor said to a Calvinist who believed in 'infant reprobation,' "Your God is my devil." We must try the spirits, whether they be of God or not, remembering that miracles can be worked by diabolism as well as by sanctity.

Emerson fails, on the whole, to differentiate between the power of holiness and the power of any kind of conscious concentration and discipline. In the essay on "Demonology," to be sure, he warns that "the best are never demonical or magnetic; leave this limbo to [Satan] the Prince of the power of the air. The lowest angel is better . . . Power as such is not known to the angels." But the warning is not frequent enough, because he did not himself need it: was not tempted by the *libido dominandi*. His 'message' — first, to himself, and then to others — is that the man of contemplation need not cringe before the man of action, as the powerless before the powerful; for meditation and contemplation are the only ultimate forms of action and hence of power.

In Emerson's formative years, he had seen the 'scholar' (his name for the 'intellectual,' whatever his mode of existence) intimidated by the seeming solidity of business and finance. He saw himself and his friends as good but powerless. Yet why were they powerless? Because, ignorant of spiritual laws, they were afraid. How absurd! Money, institutions, and buildings, though they seem ultimate realities, are but the incarnations — or, if you will, the petrified incarnations — of ideas and faith. Said Voltaire — the quotation is Emerson's — " 'tis the misfortune of worthy people that they are cowards." Deeply aware of that from self-analysis and observation, Emerson had as his mission not to denounce the powerfully evil but to remove ignorant fear from the "powerless-feeling" men of good will — to give them faith and courage and power.

He might find a "problem" in the role of Jeremy Taylor as priest and bishop, but he learned (whether from Taylor or experience) the Bishop's secret of contentedness: "If you covet learning, you must have leisure and a retired life . . . The dispersed excellencies and blessings of many men, if given to one, would not make a handsome but a monstrous fortune . . ."

Learning (as the Germans of his time understood it) and rigorously systematic thinking were vocations to which he did not feel called. He lacked the *Sitzfleisch* to spend twelve, fourteen hours a day at his books. But he was 'called' to be 'man thinking,' and a man thinking out his own problems. As Kenneth Burke says of Emerson's admirer, William James, "how profoundly . . . he earned every thing he wrote. For he wrote what was necessary to sustain him."

It isn't merely institutions that Emerson breaks away from — institutions with their economic and social security. It is also reliance on Learning and Tradition, on Books and Libraries (the intellectual equivalents of institutions). "Self-Reliance" and "The American Scholar" denounce the authority of the classic books: denunciation absurdly unnecessary to most young Americans, who never think of listening seriously to books or teachers. Emerson is addressing himself, a Harvard man descended from a clerical line.

"The American Scholar," delivered at Harvard in 1837, is but the first of Emerson's appeals to university and college students to become not mere, or merely, competent academics but 'intellectuals' — men thinking.

In 1838, he lectures on "Literary Ethics" at Dartmouth; in 1841, at Colby College, Maine, on "The Method of Nature"; in 1863, he is again at Colby, speaking on "The Man of Letters"; in 1867, he delivers an 'oration' before the Washington and Jefferson Societies at the University of Virginia — his title, "The Scholar."

Though he is addressing college classes, Emerson doesn't think of his 'scholars' as being clergymen or university professors, though of course they may become such. When he thought of scholars, I suppose he thought of Alcott, Thoreau, Brownson, Theodore Parker — rather than of George Ticknor. The 'scholar' was already on his way out of institutions — though Emerson would certainly have admitted of William James, and Santayana, probably also of Royce, and certainly of Babbitt. The "scholar, or speculative man" is his gloss in the late lecture at the University of Virginia. The scholar is the thinker, the theorist (in large contrast to the material producer: farmer and craftsmen in wood and pottery and iron and steel; mother and cook — and to the entrepreneur: banker and shopkeeper and mill-owner). Is the 'scholar' also the man of learning? Yes; but the man of more learning than original intellection is an inferior scholar, perhaps even a travesty.

Emerson and Thoreau both put impressively and intimidatingly the challenge to the intellectual, or contemplative, or 'scholar.' He must be able to live with his social conscience, must be able to face the hand workers of the world — without cringing, or feeling that he is a cripple who has adopted a cripple's job of selling spiritual shoelaces. "A sentence should read as if its author, had he held a plow instead of a pen, could have drawn a furrow deep and straight to the end": this from Thoreau. And from Emerson, addressing the young 'scholars' of Virginia: if the scholar "is not kindling his torch or collecting oil, he will fear to go by a workshop; . . . the steam engine will reprimand, the steam-pipe will hiss at him; he cannot look a blacksmith in the eye; in the field he will be shamed by mowers and reapers."

There are wrong ways of meeting this challenge: one is the attractive theory of the Brook Farmers that the scholar must transcend by including the practical man — a theory to be honored as a 'counsel of perfection.' Another, familiar to our century, is the endless quest of the neurotic intellectual to prove, in one 'line' after another, that he is able to compete — proving to himself over and over that he can do what he doesn't, centrally, want to do: as though Emerson had felt that he must prove he could professionally carry on all the chief occupations of the Yankee farmer — in garden and hay-field and cow linter — before being free to start making his career as a writer. Emerson's solid achievement of making his fellow townsmen admire him as their chief citizen was based not upon his outdoing them as a farmer but upon his integrity as a contemplative worker who had faith in his "inner working," who worked as hard and honestly as they.

FÉNELON AMONG THE
ANGLO-SAXONS

One outer wall of the Boston Public Library is incised
with the names of the doctors and saints of oecumenical
Christendom. Boston Unitarianism is represented by
W. E. Channing and Theodore Parker, leaders of the
right and left 'wings'; Eastern Orthodoxy by Origen and
St. John Chrysostom; the pre-Reformation Catholic
Church of the West by Sts. Augustine and Aquinas —
the two polar Doctors. Among the others stand the
names of the two French opponents, Bossuet and Fénelon, one above the other, but separated by the name of
Tillotson, the rationalizing Archbishop of Canterbury
during the Restoration. The arrangement of these three
seems odd; but, in view of Fénelon's status in Boston,
one can suppose him taken not as a 'full' or dogmatic
Catholic, but, like Tillotson, a minister to all, including
Unitarians.

FÉNELON AMONG THE ANGLO-SAXONS

It is not among my temptations to comprehend the whole of Fénelon's writings, or indeed to deal with them as 'literature.' Some of his pieces, like the *Télémaque* and the *Letter to Members of the Academy*, belong to the French pedagogic repertory and to the history of prose style and literary theory; others, like the opuscule on *Proofs of the Existence of God*, are graceful expositions of the sound but commonplace. It is in the *Spiritual Letters* that Fénelon has continued to live, and only with them that I am concerned.

In these, he follows a great French tradition, that of the 'spiritual director,' often not the priest-confessor of his 'patient,' sometimes even a devout layman: the director of souls who, psychologist quite as much as a theologian, deals with men and women one by one, adjusting doctrine to temperament, a sensitive dealer in 'cases of conscience.'

Fénelon's name appears in theological history as the proponent of Quietism, a form of mysticism stressing the passivity of the soul in the presence of Grace, in contrast to the popular stress upon winning merit in the eyes of God by one's good works. It is, one may say, a form of Augustinianism.

The second doctrine of Fénelon's is certainly not unrelated. Customary motives for religion, or religious behavior — the fear of hell-fire, the desire to win a not very spiritually conceived Heaven — were to him an elementary, one might even say crude, form of Christianity. Though he never quotes the hymn of St. Francis Xavier, he too can say:

> My God, I love thee not because
> I hope for Heaven thereby
> Nor yet because if I do not
> I must forever die.

We must love God for Himself alone, not for any of His goods or His special graces. The "pure love" of Fénelon can go so far as to affirm, "If God were to will to send the souls of the just to hell — as Sts. Chrysostom and Clement suggest — souls [united to God in the highest earthly state] would not love Him less."

Fénelon does not presume to hold that "mixed love" — love inclusive of self-interest — is sin; but, remembering Jesus' injunction "Be ye perfect" and His words to the rich young ruler who had kept all these moral commandments from his youth up, yet felt disquieted and incomplete, he stresses the maximal sanctity.

I dare say many of Fénelon's difficulties, his controversy with Bossuet, and the condemnation of his *Maximes des saints* by the Pope, would have been avoided had he been the director, not of men and women of 'quality,' living as lay folk in the world, but of monks and nuns. As it was, he could be represented, like the Jansenists (Catholic Puritans), as holding, for all men, standards of impracticable rigor.

Bossuet, Fénelon's opponent, certainly had 'mixed motives' in the controversy; but, one must concede, he represented the sensible administrative policy: that to present to the millions so transcendent an ideal as "pure love" is so perfectionist that it may, and doubtless will, simply alienate the masses from such religion as they are capable of. Fénelon, meanwhile, addresses himself to choice and chosen souls who, should they fail to elect the higher way, will fall below the humanistic Christianity of which all men are capable.

The greatness, the supple strength of Fénelon, as is everywhere apparent in the *Spiritual Letters*, is his combination of the eagle and the dove. Doctrinally and disciplinarily rigorous, in tone and style he is lucid, gracious, tender, affectionate — never official or pontifical. The memoirist, Saint-Simon, who admired his brilliance, distrusted him as unsimple (the kind of judgment Kingsley made of Newman); but another judgment, my own, makes him the Pauline apostle, willing to be all things to all men, if by any means he may save some.

His consanguinity with the Jesuits lies in his extraordinary skill at case-psychology — in his ability to deal with each person in terms of that person's temperament and situation. Though Fénelon's doctrine never varies, he is infinitely capable of adjusting his counsel to a particular correspondent; and, rigorous as he may be, he has infinite patience and *douceur*. He is, as Aldous Huxley rightly calls him, a Proust of spiritual psychology. English readers will find his closest counterpart in Newman; yet Newman never had, I think, the tenderness and suppleness, the complete devotion to the office of 'spiritual director' — that eminently French vocation — which was Fénelon's.

Fénelon is true to the spirit of his confessed master, St. Francis de Sales, in urging upon his aristocrats who live in society that they shall practice no ostentatious asceticism, shall participate in the harmless amusements of their world, shall discharge the responsibilities of the station in which it has pleased God to place them. It is possible, he teaches, so to cultivate the spirit of prayer that, in the midst of practical offices or proper gaieties, we can be inwardly in a state of contemplation. The *unum necessarium* is to surrender oneself totally to God — to become really humble, that is, really docile, to His voice.

Fénelon is a masterly analyst of the many ways men have of escaping God, fleeing Him down the nights and down the days, fleeing Him through 'book-religion' or the multiplicity of practical duties. He exposes the 'scrupulous' who exhaust themselves in details, and the self-conceived ascetics who assign their own disciplines instead of accepting those which befall them through God's providence. Indeed, he is a master at unmasking the innumerable modes of illusion by which men cling to their self-love. "Though I speak with the tongues of men and of angels . . . ; though I give all my goods to feed the poor . . . ; though I give my body to be burned . . ." What good works and works of supererogation won't, indeed, men assume if they can but choose their own? Yet self-elected crosses are forms of Stoicism or exhibitionism. The Christian cross confronts us as assignation, not election: as Fénelon often says, we must go forth like Abraham, not knowing whither we are to go.

His humility is as notable as the subtlety of his psychological analysis. Like Pascal and William Law, he uses his subtlety (the product, surely, of dissecting his own modes of evading God) to the end of pressing his readers to redemptive decision. Kierkegaard, and even St. Augustine and Dr. Newman, have the effect of making their readers proud of being subtle enough to follow them. Fénelon, like the author of the *Imitation of Christ*, tempts one to no such intellectual pride. Never ceasing to convey the sense that he is a gentleman whose simplicity is not naïveté but the work of Grace, Fénelon's whole effect is, with a gentleman's gentleness, to humble the intellectually proud and to make all learning seem nothing save as it ministers to spiritual growth.

Fénelon died in 1715. His first biographer — not without significance — was a Briton converted to Catholicism by Fénelon; and when, in 1728, Andrew M. Ramsay returned to Britain, he was (though a Catholic) awarded two honorary degrees by Oxford — Dr. King of St. Mary's House offering as adequate 'brief' that the candidate was an alumnus of the Archbishop of Cambrai. But English and Americans of all persuasions — not only Catholics but Anglicans, Methodists, Congregationalists, Swedenborgians, Unitarians — early accepted Fénelon as of the 'soul' of the universal Church. The very 'Quietism' which aroused the ire of Bossuet may be supposed Fénelon's recommendation to devout non-Catholics. As against Jansenism, and as against certain forms of institutional and dogmatic religion — it could be interpreted as 'mysticism' and even as the 'Inner Light.'

Thus the Quakers early saw Fénelon as an ally. In 1813, an English Quaker, William Backhouse, published *A Guide to True Peace, or A Method of Attaining to Inward and Spiritual Prayer*, chiefly compiled from the writings of Fénelon, Mme Guyon, and Molinos (the Spanish 'founder' of 'Quietism'). In his *Later Periods of Quakerism*, Rufus Jones of Haverford asserts that "there can be no question that their [Guyon's and Fénelon's] writings and especially the *Autobiography* of Mme Guyon had a marked effect upon Friends both in England and America" and that Fénelon's letters show "the rare sanity of his spiritual counsel."

John Kendall, a Quaker who published in Philadelphia (1804) *Extracts from the Writings of Fénelon*, seems, like some of Fénelon's other editors, to have thought the archbishop a near-Protestant or 'fellow-traveller.' He supposes him to believe that "the ceremonies and priesthood [of practicing Catholics like the archbishop] are but salutary aid to succor our weakness . . . Very soon these means shall cease, the shadows shall disappear, and the true temple be opened."

Such a view of Fénelon can be comprehended if one represents him by *Extracts* or makes tolerant admissions. Like 'holy' George Herbert across the channel, Fénelon was certainly one of the most oecumenical of churchmen, but there is no least reason to suppose the disciple of St. Francis de Sales not a sound Catholic. Certain propositions from his book *Maxims of the Saints* were reluctantly condemned by the Pope; but the Archbishop immediately submitted, was never excommunicated, and died, with every evidence of peace and faith, in the Catholic Church.

The first theologian who, by knowledge and sympathy, introduced the Quietists into America was Edwards, who, a few years before his death, became acquainted with *The Philosophical Principles of Natural and Revealed Religion* (1747) by Ramsay.

Here follows a significant *catena*. Of Edwards' two chief disciples, we know that Emmons copied extracts from Fénelon into a commonplace book and that Hopkins (in the tradition of the Quietists) made it a test of true Christianity to be "willing to be damned for the glory of God," characteristically preaching in Newport Parish from Romans 9:3: "For I could wish myself accursed from Christ for my brethren."

And then follows the frail and saintly William Ellery Channing, who, reared in Newport, was deeply impressed by Dr. Hopkins, "this stern teacher" who turned my "thoughts and heart to the claims and majesty of *impartial universal benevolence*." Where have we heard that unmistakable language before? And this from Channing, who, though to his death unwilling to call himself or his church 'Unitarian,' was recognized and venerated by all Boston as the real founder and real saint of what others called by that name.

FÉNELON AMONG THE ANGLO-SAXONS

The Edwardeans (with whom Channing had more in common than with Emerson and Parker) were clear on this point: they were theocentric. "The doctrines of God; absolute sovereignty and free grace, in shewing mercy to whom he would shew mercy; and man's absolute dependence on the operations of God's Holy Spirit, have often appeared to me as sweet and glorious doctrines . . . God's sovereignty has appeared to me part of this glory." Thus concludes Edwards' "Personal Narrative" — after narrating earlier that "from my childhood up, my mind had been full of objections against the doctrine of God's sovereignty, in choosing whom He would to eternal life, and rejecting whom He pleased, and to be everlastingly tormented in Hell."

Mrs. Follen, wife of the refugee Professor of German at Harvard, published in 1829 *Selections . . . with Memoir . . . by a Lady*. The first edition carried a preface by Henry D. Sedgwick; the fourth, "Introductory Remarks" by William Ellery Channing, signed March 1841.* In their course, Channing remarks that "it is the peculiarity of his [Fénelon's] reputation that it is as great among Protestants as among Catholics"; and again, "His simple words (and who is so simple?) penetrate to the depths of the soul."

Already, Channing had reviewed the first edition for the *Christian Examiner*, the official Unitarian periodical. It is probably to Channing, the unavowed leader and acknowledged saint of the Unitarians, that Fénelon owed his wide circulation among Boston Arians and Transcendentalists. His review-essay is far too rambling and

---

* The preface to *Thoughts on Spiritual Subjects, Translated from the Writings of Fenelon* (Boston, 1843) speaks of Mrs. Follen's selections as having made Fénelon's "spiritual writings . . . extensively known among us . . ."

diffuse, and reserved in its praise; but it has the merit of contrasting the *Selections* with pious books generally as an "attractive and quickening work on practical religion," and praises Fénelon as, "though a Catholic . . . , essentially free," as obviously writing "from experience," with "the great charm [of his writing] coming fresh from the soul."

Channing's is the old kind of judicial essay expositing first the faults and then the virtues of the author under discussion. On the negative side, he accuses Fénelon of taking too somber a view of human nature, though he is willing to set that down partly to the priest's early conversance with the court of Louis XIV and its intrigues (so brilliantly described in the *Memoirs* of Saint-Simon), and partly to the almost unavoidable vocational malady of the priest, who — as confessor — deals with men's sins, as the physician deals with their diseases.

Channing deplores Fénelon's making human perfection consist in "self-crucifixion." But it appears that the difference between these two saintly men is chiefly semantic. Channing, who thinks "self-respect" at least as necessary to virtue as self-denial, supposes "self-love" to be a synonym for self-respect, and hence not to be renounced. Yet surely Channing misunderstood Fénelon. The ambiguity lies in the word *self* and its compounds. Channing was thinking in terms of the New England controversy between Calvinists and liberals — the opposition between a divine tyrant good only in the *equivocal* sense that whatever He wills is good, and a univocal conception which finds God good only in the same sense we apply the term to men. About the *univocality* of man's goodness and God's, Fénelon has no doubt. Nor does Fénelon, anywhere in his *Spiritual Letters*, teach a Quietism which absorbs the individual soul in God — a Quietism either pantheistic or disjunct from 'devout humanism.'

For Fénelon, "self-love" is selfishness, not "self-respect" — the dominance of the evil, the God-fleeing and God-opposing self. In reply to Channing, Fénelon would certainly say that "self-respect," as well as peace of soul, is, by the nature of spiritual law, denied to the selfish man. It is not the 'self' as such which is opposite to God but sin, that is, the self defying spiritual law.

Emerson has his own saints — his catena of dead and living archetypes: Fénelon, a 'natural' for him, is referred to as early as the *Journals* of 1830, quoted out of Spence's *Anecdotes* from Chevalier Ramsay. In the same volume he writes that much can be learned from studying the history of the Enthusiasts. If they had, with their moral powers, "trained all their intellectual powers, they would have been wise, devout men — Newtons, Fénelons, Channings." In the same volume of the *Journals*, in 1831, he writes that "to a philosophical infidel the writings of Thomas à Kempis, of Fénelon, of Scougal, should be shown."

Emerson never lost his devotion to Fénelon. As an old man, visiting Williams College in 1865, he said — even if with diminished ardor — to an undergraduate, Charles Woodbury, "Here on your shelf is Fénelon. Who can make his pale Fénelonism but he?" This is an example of Emerson's emphasis on every man's having his own vocation; indeed the comments on Fénelon directly follow Emerson's generalization that "each man and woman is born with an aptitude to do something impossible to any other."

Doubtless the vogue of Quietism among the Transcendentalists was in some measure incited by Emerson. Thus, the Unitarian minister of Concord, the Reverend

A. W. Jackson, quotes Mme Guyon in his book on the greatest English Unitarian theologian, *James Martineau* (1900); and Louisa Alcott lists the same 'prophetess' as one of her favorite readings.

One of the chief spreaders of mysticism in general and Quietism in particular was Thomas C. Upham (1799–1872), Professor of Mental and Moral Philosophy at Bowdoin College from 1824–67. In all, he wrote sixty books, including a devotional classic, widely influential, *Principles of the Interior or Hidden Life* (1843). His remarkably bold and original work, posthumously published as *Absolute Religion* (1873), promulgates the doctrine, extraordinary among Congregationalists, of Sancta Sophia, or the Motherhood within the Divine. This doctrine appears in Catholicism and Eastern Orthodoxy, and among the Shakers and Christian Scientists ("Father-Mother God"): but it is surprising to find Upham able to cite that sturdy Boston Unitarian, Theodore Parker, as announcing the Divine Nature as "being Motherhood as well as Fatherhood." Two of Upham's other books are lives and meditations upon the lives of Catholic mystics: *Madame Guyon* (1847), and *Madame Catharine Adorna* (1845), that is, St. Catherine of Genoa.

Upham is a curiously isolated figure. Without doubting Rufus Jones's statements concerning the extent of Upham's influence, one is left with no notion of how this Congregational professor came by his remarkable range of speculative theology and knowledge of the classics of earlier mysticism. *Principles of the Interior or Hidden Life* quotes William Law's *Spirit of Prayer*, St. Francis de Sales, George Fox, Tauler (Meister Eckhart's disciple), and Jacob Boehme — as well as Fénelon. Prima-

FÉNELON AMONG THE ANGLO-SAXONS

rily, his alliance is with the French Quietists; but his early use of the phrase "disinterested or pure love," and his affirmation of 1843 that "some eminent theologians of this country appear decidedly to favor the view [of Fénelon] that the true manner of loving our neighbor is to love him in and for God," suggest certainly that his knowledge of the mystics, and his first doctrinal alliance, began with Dr. Hopkins and his followers — that is, with the Edwardeans — though, in character, he is not a dialectician as they are, and though, once finding his vocation, he is much more widely read, in Catholic as well as Protestant mystics, and much more speculative in his religious thought.

It was scarcely to be expected that American Catholics would allow Fénelon to be appropriated as really not a Catholic who died in the Faith; and, accordingly, it was inevitable that he should occasionally be overtly reclaimed. In 1864, P. O'Shea of New York published *Reflections and Meditations from the Writings of Fénelon* with an Introduction by the Reverend Thomas Preston. Fr. Preston graciously acknowledges the pleasure of Catholics that, lacking 'spiritual letters' and devotional and mystical works of their own, "the works of our masters of the spiritual life are placed in the hands of Protestants"; but he reminds his readers that such a student of à Kempis or Fénelon "will soon be led to seek the foundations on which such *moral* structures have been built," that no "theology of *negations* could mature and support any really *saintly* character." The spiritual writings of the great Archbishop, says Fr. Preston, "have been translated and circulated with eagerness, as if there could be found in them some *indirect attack* against our holy religion." But "the opponents of the

Catholic Church could find no better adversary than Fénelon, and no life more opposed to their teaching than his."

In England, Fénelon has continued to have his Catholic disciples, though, in contrast to Fr. Preston, they have not engaged in polemics against Anglicans or Protestants. The Catholic Bishop Hedley edited the *Spiritual Letters* in 1892; Lady Amabel Kerr edited, for the Catholic Truth Society, an admirable manual, *Spiritual Counsels from the Letters of Fénelon* (1905); Wilfrid Ward, son of 'Ideal Ward,' had with him on his deathbed Mrs. Lear's translation, *Letters to Men*. The scholar-saint Baron Friedrich von Hügel — who, like the man he was writing about, was oecumenical as well as Catholic — wrote to a correspondent that "[Fénelon] is one of the, say, half dozen of the non-Scriptural writers who have helped me most directly, and most copiously in my own interior life — a life requiring immensely that daily, hourly death to self."

Perhaps the most viable translations of Fénelon ever to be issued in English are the small, inexhaustible volumes, *Letters to Men* and *Letters to Women*, published at some undated time toward the end of the nineteenth century. Mrs. Henrietta Louisa Sidney Lear was, though an Anglican, a prolific translator and editor of French 'spiritual writers' and French spirituality. Characteristic among her own books are biographies of Bossuet, St. Francis de Sales, her *Fénelon . . . A Biographical Sketch* (1877), and her *Revival of Priestly Life in the Seventeenth Century in France* (1877), a monograph on the French order of Oratorians.

It goes without saying that Anglo-Catholic Evelyn Underhill (Mrs. Stuart Moore) knew and was devoted to Fénelon. In *The Mystics of the Church*, she has written what seems to me the soundest judgment of the relation between Mme Guyon and Fénelon: "It is one of the puzzles of religious history that this well-meaning, but certainly self-deluded, preacher of mysticality managed to persuade the exquisite scholar and skilled director of souls that she was indeed a prophetess and a saint." Yet, "From the retirement in which his last sixteen years were spent, Fénelon, spiritualized by adversity, wrote the greater number of those 'letters of direction,' full of wise and skilled advice on the life of love and prayer, by which he still continues his influence on souls."

We turn back to America; where, it is to be noted, Fénelon — in my judgment, a far more objective theologian and far more elegantly simple writer than Mme Guyon — has had an especial attraction for devout women.

In 1874, A. M. James, evidently an Anglican, published a translation of *Christian Counsels*. In 1877, M.W.T. (Mary W. Tileston) published, in the Boston 'Wisdom Series,' *Selections from Fénelon*, based chiefly, for the *Spiritual Letters*, on the translations of her two other notable predecessors, Mrs. Follen and Mrs. Lear.

In 1945, an Anglican, Mrs. Mildred Whitney Stillman published at the Idlewild Press, Cornwall-on-Hudson, the *Spiritual Letters of . . . Fénelon*, a small book of a hundred and twenty-two pages. Mrs. Stillman says that, to the best of her knowledge, earlier translations of her author are long since out of print, and that indeed all since "the original French edition of 1858" have been excerpts: "Excerpts in French with the imprimatur of a Roman Catholic Bishop, with Quietism left out; excerpts in English by a Boston Unitarian [Mrs. Follen] with Catholicism left out; and more recently excerpts by an Anglican [Mrs. Lear] with the atmosphere of Versailles left out." This shrewd note is accompanied by a Foreword of the Reverend Charles F. Whiston, Professor of Theology at the Church [Episcopal] Divinity School of the Pacific at Berkeley, who speaks of having for many years lent his own copies of Fénelon to readers, readers who "have been powerfully blessed."

Two years later, Mrs. Stillman and Professor Whiston again collaborated, though *Christian Perfection*, published not by a private press but by Harpers, makes no mention of the earlier book.

Mrs. Stillman translated from the 1858 (Lefevre) edition; Whiston checked it with the *Oeuvres* published by Lebel in Paris. There is a certain suggestion that the collaborators stood in some such relation as Mme Guyon and Fénelon.

I know of no other work which exalts Fénelon as Professor Whiston does — in effect, canonizing him, acclaiming him not only as saintly but a saint, a status not as yet given him by the Catholic Church. The book is formally dedicated to the "saintly" Fénelon; and Whiston affirms that the collaborators believe that Fénelon has, from his heavenly kingdom of God, been following, with his concern and intercession, "our humble attempts to make again available to people of our own age his high spiritual teaching." More, the reader is instructed to begin his reading with invocation: "Pray in this wise: O God, grant that I may sit humbly at the feet of Thy servant Fénelon, and be taught by him of Thee, his Lord and mine . . . Thus all your reading of this book will be *prayed-reading* . . . Gradually over the years this saint can become one of your deepest spiritual friends, given you of God."

Whiston's rhetoric would have been distasteful to the elegantly simple Fénelon; but it cannot be doubted that this good American has been possessed by the Fénelonian *spirit*.

If Franklin represents one persistent kind of Yankee, there is, as Mrs. Stowe observed in *Oldtown Folks*, a rival succession — the succession exemplified by the sons of Plato and of Fénelon: President Edwards, Channing, Emerson, Upham — a line not yet ended nor (*me judice*) to be ended till the Lord's Kingdom comes; till, in a quotation from St. Paul ever present in Fénelon's soul and letters, the petition be fulfilled "*ut sit DEUS omnia in omnibus.*"

"FATHER'S IDEAS":
THE ELDER HENRY JAMES

The writing went on to the end. James's family found "the sense of him, each long morning, at his study table either with bent considering brow or with a half-spent and checked intensity, a lapse backward in his chair and a musing lift of perhaps troubled and baffled eyes," the most constant fact. "He applied himself there with a regularity and a piety as little subject to sighing abatements or betrayed fears as if he had been working under pressure for his bread and ours and the question were too urgent for his daring to doubt."

There he sat at his desk, composing his papers as though the world were seriously eager for them, and revising and correcting as though competent judges were to pass them in review. It is incredible that he did not generally write rapidly and with fervor; but Henry recalls his now and then leaning back from his desk, "again and again, in long fits of remoter consideration, wondering, pondering sessions into which I was more often than not moved to read . . . some story of acute inward difficulty amounting for the time to discouragement."

He wrote facing the window, "separated but by a pane of glass . . . from the general human condition he was so devoutly concerned with. He *saw* it, through the near glass, saw it in such detail and with such a feeling for it that it broke down nowhere — that was the great thing; which truth it confirmed that his very fallings back and long waits and stays and almost stricken musings witnessed exactly to his intensity, the intensity that would 'come out,' after all, and make his passionate philosophy and the fullest array of the appearances that couldn't be blinked fit together and harmonise."

His patient and inspired work brought him "throughout the long years no ghost of a reward in the form of pence, and could proceed to publicity, as it repeatedly did, not only by the copious and resigned sacrifice of such calculations, but by his meeting in every single case all the expenses of the process."

The books met small understanding. A few reviewers, James Freeman Clarke, George Howison, C. S. Peirce, Mrs. Orr in the *Athenaeum*, took the trouble to read painstakingly and sympathetically; but few real disciples made themselves known, though these few, chiefly women, gave him really intelligent hearing and thereby much comfort: his correspondence with them was, William thinks, "perhaps his principal solace and recreation." Some of these voluble correspondences survive, notably that with Julia Kellogg, whose brochure, *The Philosophy of Henry James*, attests to her understanding of her friend's thought. The letters exhibit the same range of interests as the books, the same blend of the most abstract thought with most personal idiom. Indeed, with James, the essay and the letter were never rigorously distinguished: *Christianity the Logic of Creation* and *Society the Redeemed Form of Man* both constitute series of letters printed with much of their informal fluency still upon them; and the unpublished letter ever strains toward the essay.

In his later years — that is, after his removal to Cambridge — James moved in the best literary society of the day. He was promptly voted a member of the Saturday Club, that distinguished group which monthly convened at the Parker House. He frequented the *salon* of Mrs. Fields. In the 'seventies, he was a member of the Chestnut Street 'Radical Club.'

The mood of the 1840's, with its eager welcome to reform, to advanced social thought, to theological iconoclasm, had passed; and, though James had never been more than a purely speculative and an altogether urbane and civilized reformer, he lived on into a world which found him essentially a survival.

Echoes linger of James's bearing in this society — his witty, paradoxical conversation, his flavor as a 'character.' He carried into public his domestic habit of saying whatever would shock and hence excite some sort of spirited reaction. Without wanting in tact and knowledge of men, he chose not to adapt himself or his remarks tactfully to the company in which he found himself, but to deliver himself copiously, explosively, as conviction or mischief might move him.

Henry recalls his "finely contentious or genially perverse impulse to carry his wares of observation to the market in which they would on the whole bring least rather than most — where his offering them at all would produce rather a flurry (there might have been markets in which it had been known to produce almost a scandal) . . ."

His *obiter dicta*, as reported by the memoir writers of the period, are everywhere characteristic. Fields inquires who wrote the review of *Substance and Shadow* for the *Examiner*. "Oh! that was *merely* Freeman Clarke," James answers; "he is a smuggler in theology and feels towards me much as a contraband towards an exciseman." He warns the company not to expect serious thought from Carlyle, who is "an artist, a wilful artist, and no reasoner. He has only genius."

On another occasion he "had gone so far as to abuse Emerson pretty well [on purely 'spiritual' grounds, of course] when the latter came in. 'How do you do, Emer-son,' he said, with his peculiar intonation and voice, as if he had expected him on the heels of what had gone before." In Mr. Alcott, he pronounced on yet another occasion, "the moral sense was wholly dead, and the aesthetic sense had never been born."

Familiar doctrines as well as persons recur: "He anticipates a change in European affairs; the age of ignorance is to pass away, and strong democratic tendencies will soon pervade Europe. The march of civilization will work its revenge against aristocratic England, he believes." — "He said society was to blame for much [*much* is moderate language for James] of the crime in it, and as for that poor young man who committed the murder at Malden, it was a mere fact of temperament or inheritance."

Once at least he occupied a pulpit — that of Dr. Clarke's Boston Church of the Disciples. Again he bore witness to the faith that was in him, denouncing ecclesiasticism and the moral law as the meanest of inventions.

Mrs. Julia Ward Howe and her children sat among his auditors; and her sixteen-year-old daughter comprehended enough of the diatribe against Phariseeism to burst out, after service, with: "Mamma, I should think that Mr. James would wish the little Jameses not to wash their faces for fear it should make them suppose that they were clean" — a comment reported to have drawn a smile from Emerson.

In his last years, Mr. James doubtless came to be remembered by the world at large — if remembered he was — rather for his associations with Emerson and Carlyle and other illustrious friends, and as the father of two gifted sons, than as a philosophical writer. The intelligent reporter for the Boston *Sunday Herald* who interviewed Mr. James a few years before his death, the obituaries which appeared in the *Transcript*, the *Nation*, and elsewhere, all convey this note.

About Carlyle and Emerson, his two most illustrious friends, there was much desire to hear; and in his last years James took advantage of this by writing lectures on both. But instead of the literary gossip desired, the public got characteristic criticisms of the men and their doctrines, outspoken and audacious estimates of venerated names, uttered not by a 'reporter' but by a judge.

James's consistent later view of Carlyle represents him as compounded of prejudice and rhetoric — rhetoric sometimes in the service of prejudice, sometimes an end in itself.

In substance, there are two indictments: that Carlyle lacked any genuine belief in humanity and that he believed in heroes, not in men. He was "deficient in spiritual as opposed to moral force." In the teeth of all the prophets who have ever prophesied, he held that the race *is* always to the swift, the battle always to the strong.

Long before Mr. Darwin had thought of applying the principle of natural selection to the animal kingdom, Carlyle, not in words but in fact, had applied it to the spiritual kingdom, proclaiming it as fundamental axiom of the divine administration.

"He had no belief in society as a living, organizing force, in history, but only as an empirical necessity of the race." He believed in the finality of the conflict between good and evil; found the conflict valid in itself, its own end; never guessed that it was merely propaedeutic to an ultimate and permanent harmony.

But worse, he was a literary man before everything else, and subordinated even the ignoble doctrine he preached to the exigencies of his personal genius. "Carlyle was, in truth, a hardened declaimer. He talked in a way vastly to tickle his auditors, and his enjoyment of their amusement was lively enough to sap his own intellectual integrity. Artist like, he precipitated himself upon the picturesque in character and manners wherever he found it, and he did not care a jot what incidental interest his precipitancy lacerated."

"You would say, remembering certain passages in Carlyle's books — notably his 'Past and Present' and his pamphlet on Chartism — that he had a very lively sympathy with reform and a profound sentiment of human fellowship. He did, indeed, dally with the divine ideas long enough to suck them dry of their rhetorical juices, but then dropped them, to lavish contempt on them ever after when anybody else should chance to pick them up and cherish them, not for their rhetorical uses, but their absolute truth."

Emerson remained the puzzle he had ever been: at once irritation and enchantment; intellectually sterile, personally altogether lovely and prophetic of the coming man. "Mr. Emerson's authority to the imagination consists, not in his culture, not in his science, but all simply in himself, in the form of his natural personality. There are scores of men of more advanced ideas than Mr. Emerson, of subtler apprehension, of broader knowledge, of deeper culture . . . Mr. Emerson was never the least of a pedagogue, addressing your scientific intelligence, but an every way unconscious prophet, appealing exclusively to the regenerate heart of mankind, and announcing the speedy fulfilment of the hope with which it had always been pregnant. He was an American John the Baptist, proclaiming tidings of great joy to the American Israel; but, like John the Baptist, he could so little foretell the form in which the predicted good was to appear, that when you went to him he was always uncertain whether you were he who should come, or another."

James was not in the least disposed, after the fashion of Matthew Arnold, to deny the Concordian the eminence of great writer: "There is no technical man of letters in the land who will not cordially bow to Mr. Emerson's literary sceptre." Emerson's "speech is colour and melody and fragrance itself to my senses." Yet he must agree with Arnold that his pre-eminence lay elsewhere. "I think it has never once occurred to me in my long intercourse with Mr. Emerson to prize his literary friendship, or covet any advantage which might accrue from it to myself. No, what alone I have sought in Mr. Emerson is not the conscious scholar, but always the unconscious prophet, whose genius, and not by any means his intellect, announces, with unprecedented emphasis, spontaneity as the supreme law of human life."

Not for what he thought or said or wrote, but for

what he was and what he adumbrated, could James be grateful. One could turn from his thought to his character, all innocent of moralism, all spontaneous, all instinct with the Divine: there one found satisfaction. His thought, like the thought of all the Transcendentalists, exalted individualism; his spirit exhibited the sweetest graces of a universal humanity.

Though Emerson, like Carlyle, had a veneration for the great, there is this profound difference in their attitude: that Carlyle makes of them heroes, set apart by their genius from our common humanity; Emerson makes of them *representative* men. "He indeed honours great men, but only for their human substance . . . they *do* represent something more than they individually constitute, and this is a great gain."

Carlyle, unknowingly, ended the old moralistic dispensation; Emerson, with equal unconsciousness, inaugurated the new. He "rings in that better world inaugurated by the second Adam, in which at last the divine spirit is supreme, and our nature, consequently touched by that inspiration, brings forth immaculate fruit; that is, all those spontaneous graces of heart and mind and manners which alone have power to redeem us to eternal innocence, peace, and self-oblivion."

The main thing about Emerson was that he "unconsciously brought you face to face with the infinite in humanity." Everything in him "seemed innocent by the transparent absence of selfhood." He "recognized no God outside of himself and his interlocutor, and recognized him there only as the *liaison* between the two, taking care that all their intercourse should be holy with a holiness undreamed of before by man or angel. For it is not a holiness taught by books or the example of tire-

81

some, diseased, self-conscious saints, but simply by one's own redeemed flesh and blood." The holiness for which Emerson lived was innocence; and innocence "attaches only to what is definitely universal or natural in our experience, and hence appropriates itself to individuals only in so far as they learn to denude themselves of personality or self-consciousness."

James's *obiter dicta* upon his other 'literary' friends possess the same freshness and downright frankness. With their strictly literary merits, he cannot, of course, bother. Without denying or even doubting them, he is ever impatient of what, to him, is purely mediatory or vehicular; he is concerned with the doctrine.

If James expressed himself with some frankness about his associates, no one would suspect him of jealousy. His largeness of nature forbade any bitterness over the difference between his modest fame and the glories which attended Emerson and Carlyle; and never thinking of himself (as indeed he had no necessity) as the inferior of his more famous friends, he had no desire to abase their reputations that his own might be exalted.

His untempered criticism was motivated partly by sincere dissent from the philosophies they represented (Transcendental individualism and Carlylian hero worship, alike offensive to a democrat), partly, perhaps principally, from the desire to rebuke the widespread taste for literary gossip and the widespread veneration for great names. To magnify 'personalities' is to make light of God's redemptive work in humanity.

"Nothing so endlessly besotted in Mr. James's eyes," writes his son William, "as the pretension to possess personally any substantive merit or advantage whatever, any worth other than your unconscious uses to your kind! Nothing pleased him like exploding the bubbles of conventional dignity, unless it was fraternizing on the simplest and lowest plane with all lowly persons whom he met."

He wrote Miss Kellogg: "The common place people you despise in comparison with Plato and Emerson are not agreeable to me on the score of any spiritual attainments they appear to have made, but only on the ground of their not exhibiting so dense an obscuration, in their proper personality, of the Divine glory. They seem to be immersed in active use, to cherish no consciousness of virtue or genius or talent or anything of that sort, and so let the Lord shine through them without any excessive clouding of his splendour. But your Platos and Emersons are somebodies in respect to these nobodies, and I accordingly who live only by trying to believe in the Lord's sole worth in humanity, and am therefore delighted always to be with self-evident nobodies, feel greatly discontented and disheartened to find that I have to deal also with these pretentious somebodies and dispose of them before I can again get a sight of the Lord ... Whenever I get my stupid sconce above water for half an hour, some of the reigning idols, Plato or Emerson or Washington, is sure to plump himself down upon it, and submerge me in the atheistic flood for another century. The people in the horse-cars never do this. They never stimulate me to show off. They never suggest to me that there [are] differences among men in themselves ... They talk so heartily of household expenses and weather and raising chickens that it is sweet to be near them."

The horse-car became at once a shrine and a symbol to James. His friend Godkin, editor of the New York

Nation, quotes him as maintaining that to a right-minded man a crowded Cambridge horse-car "was the nearest approach to Heaven on earth."

In *Society the Redeemed Form of Man,* James pays his devotions at the same shrine. Under the grand heading, "The Horse-Car our True Shechinah at This Day," he confesses to the "frankly chaotic or a-cosmical aspect of our ordinary streetcar," only to avow, "I nevertheless continually witness so much mutual forbearance on the part of its *habitués;* so much spotless acquiescence under the rudest personal jostling and inconvenience; such a cheerful renunciation of one's strict right; such an amused deference, oftentimes, to one's invasive neighbor: in short, and as a general thing, such a heavenly self-shrinkage in order that 'the neighbor,' handsome or unhandsome, wholesome or unwholesome, may sit or stand at ease: that I not seldom find myself inwardly exclaiming with the patriarch: *How dreadful is this place! It is none other than the house of God, and the gate of heaven!*"

James's wife died in February 1882, and the 'philosopher' survived her only till December. His strength had been gradually fading for some time; and his "general mental powers were visibly altered" during the last year, but not so his grasp of his philosophy. His son William testifies: "His truths were his life; and when all else had ebbed away, his grasp of them was still vigorous and sure."

A week before he died, his daughter Alice asked for directions about his funeral. "He was immediately very much interested, not having apparently thought of it before; he reflected for some time, and then said with the greatest solemnity and looking so majestic: 'Tell him to say only this: Here lies a man, who has thought all his life that the ceremonies attending birth, marriage and death were all damned non-sense. Don't let him say a word more.' "

Another 'dying remark' is equally vehement but, in contrast, an affirmative: "I stick by Almighty God — He alone *is:* all else is death. Don't call this dying; I am just entering upon life."

In 1885, William edited, as his own first publication, a volume of his father's last writing. Despite the title, with its archaism and grotesque treason to the spirit of his father, the introduction to *The Literary Remains* is an admirably perceptive essay.

Thus William of his father: "Whenever the eye falls upon one of Mr. James's pages — whether it be a letter to a newspaper or to a friend, whether it be his earliest or his latest book — we seem to find him saying again and again the same thing; telling us what the true relation is between mankind and its Creator. What he had to say on this point was the burden of his whole life, and its only burden. When he had said it once, he was disgusted with the insufficiency of the formulation (he always hated the sight of his old books), and set himself to work to say it again. But he never analysed his terms or his data beyond a certain point, and made very few fundamentally new discriminations; so the result of all these successive re-editings was repetition and amplification and enrichment, rather than reconstruction. The student of any one of his works knows, consequently, all that is *essential* in the rest."

A young author feels compelled to compress into his first book a complete transcription. James never outgrew this adolescent prodigality. Besides all that he had felt and thought upon the secret of the universe, he had views upon all lesser themes: crime, poverty, wealth, waste; marriage and the 'woman question'; Swedenborg and the Swedenborgians; spiritualism; art; metaphysics. Instead of devoting a book to each of his interests, he devotes every book — nay, every magazine essay — to all of them. Whatever the announced topic — Woman, Crime, Spiritualism — we presently find ourselves carried inevitably into the theory of Creation.

James's earlier writings were largely occupied with negative criticisms of religious orthodoxy, both Evangelical and Swedenborgian; and his later works never weary of defining their position by its contrariety to current views in philosophy and science as well as religion. But combat is no longer their prime motive. Their 'superficial polemics' never disturb the central peace which pervades them.

James published four full portraitures of his mind: *Christianity the Logic of Creation* (1857), *Substance and Shadow* (1863), *The Secret of Swedenborg* (1869), *Society the Redeemed Form of Man* (1879); and during the last year of his life he was revising the proof of a fifth, *Spiritual Creation* (1882). The first of these is the most succinct; but the later formulations are not only, as William James thought, philosophically the best but the best written as well. 'Best' for both philosophy and style must be interpreted as *most characteristic of James*. He felt only disgust for the 'personal' and wanted, like a proper philosopher, to enunciate what was true not for him but for all men. His whole turn of mind and idiom set him apart alike from the philosophers and the men of letters of his day. He was too much of a dialectician to turn *littérateur*, but he balked at limiting himself to ratiocination. He argues; and wearying of argument, he turns to striking example, pungent satire, eloquent apostrophe, prophetic declaration. For all his fond addiction

86

to verbal distinctions, he uses his terms freely, not consistently.

James's style at his most characteristic deserves the high praise which has so abundantly been awarded it, not for organization — that James lacked, was impatient of — but for style in the romantic sense: for diction in turn learned and homely, incomparably varied and rich and living; sentences sharpened to aphorism; paragraphs which work to a climax; longer sequences in which the author feels emotionally moved by his own argument and loses himself in its poetry.

Best, as thus defined — that is, most characteristic of their author, most rich in the display of his powers of humor, eloquence, perception — are *The Secret of Swedenborg, Society the Redeemed Form of Man*, and *Spiritual Creation*. Grand books these: America has produced nothing else like them; but Mark Twain, Melville, and Whitman — rather than Emerson or Hawthorne — are James's congeners.

To come to the philosophy itself. It must first be inquired how we apprehend truth, as distinguished from sense perception and 'fact.' Suppose (in Swedenborgian allegory and diction) that God is pleased to call His children out of Egypt, and its 'scientifics,' its memory-knowledge, into the Promised Land of spiritual wisdom: how will He effect it?

Not by theology, with its myth and dogma; not by metaphysics (*God is not pleased to save his people by dialectic*); not by science, with its limitation to fact and the phenomenal, James answers, but by Philosophy. For philosophy — true philosophy, that is — operates by perception. It attends to the voice of the heart; to race instinct, vaguer and deeper yet; to *the hidden God*.

"Science confines herself only to phenomena and their relations, that is, to what is strictly verifiable in some sort by sense; and so stigmatizes the pursuit of being or substance as fatal to her fundamental principles. Philosophy, in short, is the pursuit of Truth, supersensuous truth, recognisable only by the heart of the race, or if by its intellect, still only through a life and power derived from the heart. Science has no eye for truth, but only for Fact, which is the appearance that truth puts on to the senses, and is therefore intrinsically second-hand, or shallow and reflective."

"Ratiocination is doubtless an honest pastime, or it would not be so much in vogue as a means of acquiring truth. But the truth we are elucidating is Divine, and therefore is great enough to authenticate itself, or furnish its own evidence."

"I shall not affront your self-respect," James assures us, "by affecting to demonstrate the truth of God's NATURAL humanity scientifically: in the first place, because it is not a fact of sense, and therefore escapes the supervision of science; and in the second place, because . . . I am anxious to conciliate your heart primarily, while your head is quite a subordinate aim. I cannot tell you a single reason, unprompted by the heart, why I myself believe the truth in question or any other truth for that matter . . . In fact, I believe it simply because I love it, or it seems adorably good to me; and once having learned to love it, I could not do without it. It would in truth kill me, intellectually, to doubt it . . . To my experience this is the only thing that in the long run authenticates truth to the intellect — *the heart's sincere craving for it.* I find that truth unloved is always at bottom truth unbelieved, however much it may be 'professed.' "

Sometimes James calls this philosophy of the heart Revelation; but in appropriating this term his point is to underscore the self-evident, primary character of religious intuition; to distinguish it from those other modes of knowledge derivative of sense perception. For the orthodox notion of Revelation, construing it as Divine deliverances of alleged historical occurrences and legal precepts, James has only scorn.

Revelation conveys to us first principles unvouchsafed by either observation or experience. There would be no object in the *revelation* of truth which could be arrived at empirically, verified by experiment. The deepest aspirations of the heart seem so palpably beyond our experience actual or possible as to disavow all phenomenal parentage. "Flesh and blood hath not revealed it unto you": that much we feel sure of. The "supremely true is never the probable." "The sphere of Revelation is the sphere of life exclusively; and its truth is addressed not to the reflective understanding of men, but to their living perception. Truth, to every soul that has ever felt its inward breathing, disowns all outward authority — disowns, if need be, all outward *probability* or attestation of Fact. The only witness it craves, and this witness it depends upon, is that of good in the heart."

'Revelation' so conceived is, of course, not subject to argument: it is primary and self-evident — its own witness. We can merely avow it, and let it make its way into the hearts of all sincerely spiritual persons upon whose attention it may impinge.

The "precious facts of revelation, whether they fall within the sphere of my understanding or my affections, quite transcend the grasp of my critical faculty, and impose themselves upon my heart as an unmixed good, which I am just as incapable of measuring in terms of the analytic intellect, or reducing to the contrast of the true and the false, as I am of demonstrating to a blind man the pleasure of a gorgeous sunset, or reasoning a man without a palate into the savor of sugar."

James's metaphysics may be called one of *Creation*, provided we are willing to give the term an ontological rather than a cosmological flavor. By this favorite word, James was far from meaning the process whereby Jehovah's *fiat* brought into time and space existence the natural world; he was not in the least troubled over the early narrative of Genesis and whether the 'six days' were twenty-four hours long or an aeon in duration or a moment.

Evolution, to him quite conceivable as a scientific hypothesis, could in no way conflict with a philosophic theory of creation, but it was intolerable that scientists and theologians alike took Nature as primary and ultimate, or 'real.' Nature is the least real of all existences, for nature is "a mere implication of man, . . . exists *in itself* only to carnal thought, or an intelligence unemancipated from sense." All that sensibly exists is "but the mind's furniture." The spiritual thought of man "makes all sensible existence to fall within the unitary mind of the race."

Nature is so far from existing in her own right as to be completely void of intrinsic substance. Nature mirrors the race mind: that is its use. Consciousness sets man off from his creator; Nature gives that consciousness the only possible ground for operation.

By imaging forth spiritual entities, natural objects acquaint the spirit of man with his own constitution. If my sensible experience "did not furnish my rational understanding with a complete livery or symbolism of abstract human nature, with an infinitely modulated key wherewith to unlock all the secret chambers of the human heart, all the infinite possibilities of character among men — I should be forever destitute of moral perception . . . ; because thought is impossible without language; and language derives all its substance or body from things, or the contents of our sensible experience."

The true creature of God is man, and God's essence is Love. Conjunction of love is the result of reciprocity, says Swedenborg in his *Sapientia Angelica;* and reciprocity can have no place in one person only. "It is clear therefore that the Divine Love cannot but be and exist in others whom it may love, and by whom it may be loved. For since such a principle is in all love, it must be specially, that is, infinitely, in Love Itself.

"As for God, it is impossible for Him to love and to be loved reciprocally in others having anything of infinity, that is, anything of the essence and life of love in itself, or anything of the Divine." In such case, God would be loving himself, for there is but one Divine Substance, one Very Reality. And of self-love, Swedenborg continues, "there cannot be the least trace in God, for it is altogether opposed to the Divine Essence."

The real Creation, then, is the creation of creatures whom God may love. God alone is Life, and He cannot create other beings having life in themselves. Yet He must in some sense project his creatures from Himself, give them, if not *being,* then at least *existence.* That the creatures should be real as God is real flouts every philosophic instinct, but they must possess at the least a sort of reality, a quasi-reality, a reality to themselves, else there is no escape from Pantheism, and God is loving not others but Himself.

Sometimes James gives the name of Creation only to the process whereby God projects us from Himself, but sometimes he makes it cover as well the return, or *redemption*, as he elsewhere calls it. Thus he says in the *Secret of Swedenborg*, "creation, philosophically viewed, involves a divided movement — one descending, generic, physical, by which the creature becomes set off, projected, alienated from the creator in mineral, vegetable, and animal form; the other ascending, specific, moral, by which the creature thus pronounced becomes *conscious of himself* as separated from his creative source, and instinctively reacts against the fact, or seeks to reunite himself with God."

But Creation is, first, projection. How is God to set the creature off from himself without either making him objectively disjunct, real as God is real — or reducing him to the mere appearance of Reality?

Taking a hint from Swedenborg, James declares that God can at most afford man only a provisional reality; man is not to possess life in himself, but merely to feel as if he possessed life in himself. He really lives in God, but he is to suppose himself acting and living "as of himself."

Is the self, then, illusory? James helps us to interpret this doctrine of the provisional self, as Swedenborg fails to do. We have, he explains, to deal with two orders, two "discrete degrees," of the real. The self is illusory only from an absolute or philosophic point of view; but just as Nature is real to the senses (illusory only when taken philosophically as possessing substance), so with the self: it is real on its own plane — that is, to consciousness.

Man, "*in so far as he is man*, does not exist to sense, but only to consciousness; and consequently human nature properly speaking is not a thing of physical but of strictly moral attributes. In so far as man exists to sense he is identical with mineral, vegetable and animal; and it is only as he exists to consciousness, that he becomes naturally differentiated or individualized from these lower forms, and puts on a truly human, which is an exclusively moral, personality."

Repeatedly, James distinguishes Creator from created as Substance from Form, Essence from Existence. God is our *esse*, as we are His *existere*. Our objectivity rests in God, while He attains to subjectivity only in us.

God neither possesses consciousness nor can be possessed by it. Human consciousness, indeed, is the wall between us and God, erected by God in order to give us a room of our own, and a wall hiding us from our benefactor.

It is in giving us this consciousness from which He is hidden, this "proud and sufficient selfhood" whereby man may "absolutely deny his maker, and search the universe in vain to find a God . . . [that] God truly creates, and how truly and completely! The Incarnation of God in man, and through man to outermost nature, is, indeed, rather to be thought of as patient suffering, as self-emptying. God took upon Him the form of a servant, not merely in Jesus, but in His whole creative work. Creation is no ostentatious self-assertion, no dazzling parade of magical, irrational, or irresponsible power; it is an endless humiliation or prorogation of [God] himself to all the lowest exigencies of the created consciousness."

God indeed so completely abases Himself, so veils His splendor from consciousness, so fears to break in upon the selfhood of his creatures, that He runs the risk of their confirming themselves in their first and perfectly natural thought that they really are what they seem to themselves to be — self-sufficient.

93

"So that practically, or in its initiament, creation takes on a wholly illusory aspect, the creature alone appearing, or claiming at most a traditional recognition."

Evil indeed comes into being along with the self. Not that the self in itself is evil: in itself it is the provisional platform for all man's subsequent moral and spiritual development; but to confirm oneself in taking it as absolute as it appears is to fall into evil.

Man once projected from God, given what possible degree of otherness God can assign him, how does the *return* effect itself? How does man reconcile himself with his creator? They have been made two on purpose that union may result, that they may be one, not by identity or legal coercion but by mutual love.

James found current two answers, *moralism* and *ecclesiasticism*, both of which he rejected as false, the more because both made arrogant pretensions to righteousness. "Who are Christ's spiritual foes, the only foes possible to him at this day? They are *friends . . . to his carnal or historic personality*. The first class may be for convenience's sake called moralistic: being made up of that very large number of persons who live and thrive in contentment with the existing very infirm constitution of society: poets, literary essayists, scholars, artists, *transcendental aspirants or idealists* [italics mine], men of science . . . : all of whom blindly regard morality as the absolute law of human life, and look upon duty as the highest expression of human character, especially for other people."

"The second class is mainly ecclesiastical, of course, and lives and thrives in safe contentment, not with this world to be sure, but with another one which by all accounts is greatly more unequal or undivine and vicious even than this. It comprises all of every sect who regard the traditional church as directly in the line of man's spiritual welfare, or as supplying by Divine appointment a literal pathway to heaven."

Of these classes, the former is of course parasitic upon the latter. Moralism is a comparatively recent disease. The Church "historically breeds, sweats, or throws off from its flanks, the civilized state of man,* and morality is the unquestionable law of civilization, the absolute substance, condition, and measure of all our civic righteousness."

Unitarianism is the movement which best represents moralism: it takes moral character and 'good works' as absolute, and as making men righteous in the sight of God. But Unitarianism still preserves, however, the semblance of a church. Outside the 'churches,' more overtly, moralism can and does flourish — as Transcendentalism, as 'ethical culture,' as philanthropy. The 'New England conscience,' with its fussy self-consciousness and self-culture and 'scrupulosity' is one of moralism's most flagrant, most neurotic, forms.

The church, however, is the basic offender. Religion was intended to wean man not merely from the 'world' but from all personal pretensions to righteousness; to assure man not of finding personal favor in the sight of God, but achieving redemption from all personal hopes and fears through solidarity with all his kind. "Religion was once a spiritual life in the earth, though a very rude and terrible one . . . "

Conscience, through which our spiritual life begins to operate, was never intended to make us self-complacent. Like the Law, its office was meant to be purely negative: to convict us of sin. James follows St. Paul in his

* James uses the word *civilized* in the contemptuous sense of Fourier, much as the Marxians use *bourgeois*.

95

indictment of legalism. The representative or formal church, alas, has often fallen into the legalism it arose to confound. It has assured men of absolute difference between saint and sinner, and given them hope of finding personal favor in God's sight.

Three sorts of religious experience are equally offensive: the Unitarian variety, which thinks of God primarily as a Divine Moral Being, who is gratified by our personal advances in ethical culture; the Catholic variety, whether Roman or Anglican, which considers right relations between God and man as essentially *ex opere operato*, ceremonially or ritually achieved; the Evangelical variety, which takes an erotic, or at any rate a sentimental, turn, and dispenses with moral and ceremonial relations only in order to substitute a purely *personal* intimacy.

James illustrates this third variety, still not extinct, by recalling a loquacious acquaintance of his who said, "I can't imagine how any one should have any distrust of God. For my part, if I were once in His presence, I should feel like *cuddling-up* to Him as instinctively as I would cuddle-up to the sunshine or fire in a wintry day." — "It is beautiful to observe," James adds, "how utterly destitute Swedenborg found the angelic mind of all this putrid sentimentality, this abject personal piety."

A fourth sort of religious experience with which he was familiar, the Calvinistic, though also "heretical," James preferred to the other three, by virtue of its virile contempt for both moralism and sentimentality and its awareness of the gulf between Creator and creature.

Only the shallow, whether within or without the church, can rest in moralism. The Law is our schoolmaster to bring us to Christ: those who most assiduously attempt to obey the Law will soonest confess their

complete insufficiency for their task, will soonest surrender to the Gospel. Conscience similarly arrests our
spiritual development at moralism only when we grow
slothful, inattentive; when we pause at partial or purely
ceremonial compliance with her precepts.

The revelation of God in Jesus Christ offers the way
out of legalism, and turns us from our self-righteousness
and Pharisaism to a life beyond good and evil, a life of
love and spontaneous brotherhood: The New Testament "addresses no inviting or soothing word of any sort
to the saint, but only to the sinner. In one of these very
rare gospel incidents which give us a glimpse into
Christ's *personal* temperament, a saintly youth presents
himself so aglow with all moral excellence, that Christ
cannot help testifying a natural impulse of affection towards him; but he nevertheless straightway charges him
to set no value upon his virtue as a celestial qualification.
'If thou wilt be *perfect*, go and *sell all that thou hast*.' "

The way out of legalism is first of all negative: to
cease piquing ourselves upon our distinctions from
others — our possessions, our virtues. How hardly shall
the man of parts, powers, personal pretensions, enter
into the Kingdom of Heaven! Progress, indeed, "whether
public or private, seems to take place in an invariably
negative way — that is, it always exacts a preliminary
experience and acknowledgement of evil and error. Our
vices and follies, collective and personal, have wrought
us infinitely more advantage than our virtue and
knowledge have ever achieved. Our best learning has
come to us in the way of unlearning our prejudice, our
best wisdom in the way of outgrowing conceit . . . So
palpably true is all this, that the fundamental grace of
the religious character throughout history is humility;

97

the primary evidence of a spiritual quickening in the soul, repentance."

At the time of Christ's Advent, "the Stoics were the leaders of speculative thought. To fall back on all occasions upon one's moral force, and find a refuge against calamity in one's native strength of will, was the best recognized wisdom of man . . . Christ probably had never heard of the Stoics, but if he had he could only have been revolted by their doctrine, since his own was the exact and total inversion of theirs. The ideal of the Stoic was rich and cultivated manhood. The ideal of Christ was innocent unconscious childhood. According to Christ, what men need in order to the full enjoyment of the divine favor is to be emptied of all personal pretension, to become indifferent to all self-seeking or self-providence . . . "

But the orthodox church has substituted for Jesus' zeal for humanity a "zeal for the person of Jesus himself." The church "makes Jesus, under the name of a mediator, a perpetual barrier to the cordial intercourse of God and man." According to its teaching, Jesus "exhausts the worth of human nature, so that no man created by God can ever appear tolerable to God, unless shining with his reflected lustre." It converts Jesus into "a monster of self-seeking" and turns "the grace of the gospel into a mere argument of his personal supremacy." We believe in his personal pretensions, or we are damned. He is indeed alleged to have done us a signal favor (dying to reconcile us to an angry God); but he then claims our worship in return, "under penalty of death, under penalty of everlasting misery. It is a purely diabolic claim, which all humanity disowns with loathing and contempt."

The Lord is Swedenborg's name for the God-Man,

God Incarnate. Refusing to identify the *Deus Homo* with the historic Jesus, James interprets the term as denoting the union of God with man. "By the Lord regarded spiritually or rationally, then, we do not mean any literal or personal man, capable of being sensibly comprehended; but we mean that Divine and universal life in man, which grows out of the conjunction of the infinite Divine Love with our finite natural love . . . "

What state, now, are we to look to as fulfilling the destiny of mankind? Moralism we know, and *civilization*, its social equivalent. The Law we know; but what then is the Gospel? How shall we conceive of the final union between God and man?

These questions James but imprecisely answers. Creation implies Redemption: James "scorned to admit, even as a possibility, that the great and loving Creator, who has all the being and the power, and has brought us as far as *this*, should not bring us *through*, and *out*, into the most triumphant harmony." But only Revelation can give us belief in such a harmony; and Revelation never discloses facts but only apocalyptic perceptions.

The state beyond moralism is spiritual Christianity; the state beyond 'civilization' is socialism; or, since socialism has come to mean a special sort of organization, we had better say Society. James looks forward to the abolition of all government — is, in short, a 'philosophical anarchist.' With St. Augustine, James says "Love, and do what you will." The State will pass away; so will the Church. Once God's living presence in Society is recognized, no representative ritual will be necessary.

Men will transcend the moral life, with its good and evil. Heaven and hell, "both alike nothing but logical, ordinary, and inevitable spiritual incidents of our *natural* or race evolution," will both finally "coalesce in that

99

final unitary display of omnipotent goodness and wisdom known as human SOCIETY, or the Lord's KINGDOM UPON EARTH."

The distinctive character of the moral life is choice; its distinctive operation is obedience to *duty*. "The element of will or choice is everything in the moral life, and the fussy votaries of it accordingly are absurdly tenacious of their personal merit. But this element of will or choice scarcely enters appreciably into the spiritual life, unless into the lowest forms of it; and in all the higher or celestial forms it is unknown." Choice will pass away in favor of spontaneity. We shall *love and do what we will*.

In some such eschatological *myth* does James conceive of the New Jerusalem: the *reality*, the essence of this consummation, will consist in the union of God with his creatures.

The question is how James conceived of God.

William's comment, that his father nowhere argues the *existence* of God, is naive in a way which William later outgrew. In the sense of denying an 'ultimate reality,' there are doubtless no atheists except "fools." It marked James's central depth that his question concerned not the *existence* but the *nature* of God. If all men are believers and worshippers, some worship power or its subdeities, money or sex — fallen angels seducing, if possible, the very elect.

Many men worship a God who is not (in Scholastic terminology) univocally good — that is, not good in the sense by which we judge our neighbors. High Calvinism clearly denies any such democracy. The test of a really devout Christian, according to Dr. Hopkins, Jonathan Edwards' disciple and successor in the development of doctrine, is his willingness to be "damned for the glory of God," a criterion as debasing of the divine as heroic in its expectation of man.

Father Taylor, the Methodist preacher, was right when he said to the Calvinists: "Your God is my Devil"; for, as the Absolute Monarch, the Divine Despot, He must of course, have ordained, before the foundation of the world that, without respect to their vices or virtues, some men shall be eternally saved and others eternally damned.

William James appears to have accepted his father as a theist. Yet his father sharply rebukes all belief in a 'personal' God, a God external to His creatures. God is not outside us — another, if greater, self. To "be a conscious person is to be self-centred, and to be God is to be not only without self-hood, but identical with universal life or being." Spiritual nearness to God "implies infinite personal remoteness from him, since God avouches himself to be universal life or being, which is flagrantly incompatible either with the fact or the sentiment of personality."

Denying that God is "a person finited from man by space and time," James affirms that God is "the inmost and inseparable life of every man great or small, wise or stupid, good or evil." Even the literal Christian verity, he thinks, "justifies us in ascribing to Him henceforth a distinctly NATURAL or impersonal infinitude, and so forever rids us both of the baleful intellectual falsities inherent in the conception of His supernatural personality, and of the enforced personal homage, precatory and deprecatory, engendered by that conception in the sphere of our sentimental piety." He avows: "I have not the least sentiment of worship for His name, the least sentiment of awe or reverence towards Him, considered as a perfect person sufficient unto Himself. That style of deity exerts no attraction either upon my heart or understanding. Any mother who suckles her babe upon her own breast, any bitch in fact who litters her periodical brood of pups, presents to my imagination a vastly nearer and sweeter Divine charm."

How, then, are we to conceive of God? Swedenborg's statement that 'God is very man' has often been translated, conformably to the presupposition of orthodox theism, into 'God is *a man*'; and orthodox Swedenborgians have construed that Jesus, or the Lord, is alone God. James, however, understands Swedenborg to mean that God is not a man, but MAN. "There is no God but the Lord, or our glorified NATURAL humanity; and whatsoever other deity we worship is but a baleful idol of our own spiritual fantasy, whom we superstitiously project into nature to scourge us into *quasi* or provisional manhood, while as yet we are blind to the spiritual truth."

"In short, my reader, if human nature, the human race, mankind, or humanity, be not *spiritually* the only true name of God, exhausting the conception, then I at least do not know the true name of God, and certainly should never care to know it."

Does James mean that God is merely universal man, a kind of Platonic Idea in which, by participation, all become men? Or is he, like Comte, urging the substitution of Humanity for God as the object of our worship? Not so. He expressly dissociated himself from Comte's doctrine; and he would require some more dynamic relationship of creator to created than that of Idea to particulars.

James, one has to believe, is sincere in rejecting the Comtean view of God as inadequate. God is more than the sum total of men, not in the least an abstraction, a generalization, an idea; for James conceives of God as active, as indeed the one really active force in the universe, the one true substance. We do not make God in our image; rather, in some deep if obscure sense, He makes us in his. No more than any Augustinian, can James believe that men's ordinary selves can effect salvation. The old theology gone, the problem of grace is still left. The "individual man, as such, is nothing, but owes all he is and has to the race nature he inherits, and to the society in which he was born." But how can there be more in the race, as such, than the sum total of our individual natures? We are not yet free from old dispute between Realist, Conceptualist, and Nominalist.

Says James: "The race alone is *real* man, and invariably sets the tune, therefore, for us paltry, personal or phenomenal men to march to. And consequently we turn out good or evil persons — that is to say, even *phenomenally* good or evil men — just as we consent or refuse to keep step with the race's music." But who sets the tune? And the real man is of course not the sum total of men, or an average of all men, but the spiritual meaning of man — what he may be when Redemption has completed its work and the kingdoms of this world have become the kingdoms of our God, and society has become the "redeemed form of man." The Real Man is a sort of Aristotelian final cause: the point of life, of history, as its End.

If we ask whether Man exhausts the meaning of God, James will perhaps tell us that God in himself is Infinite Love and Infinite Wisdom. Further, "He of all beings is the *least* free, has the *least* power, to act arbitrarily, or follow his own caprice . . . " But God in Himself we cannot know: we can know only the Lord, the God-Man or "the infinite Divine love and wisdom in union with every soul of man." In short, James denies a 'personal' God outside of humanity, conceives of God as the creative principle within humanity.

Can such a world view be called Christian? William James confesses inability "to see any radical and essential necessity for the mission of Christ in his [father's] scheme of the universe. A 'fall' there is, and a redemption; but . . . I cannot help thinking that if my father had been born outside the pale of Christendom, he might perfectly well have brought together all the other elements of his system, much as it stands now . . . " Neo-Platonism suggests the *lapse* and the *return;* Fourier and Comte suggest a democratic socialism, not hostile to some ritual version of their doctrines.

But neo-Platonism is a Gnostic way for 'intellectuals'; and, on the other hand, James's God is something other than Comte's, as James's philosophy transcends the sort of positivistic socialism he found about him.

Toward the end of his life he confessed himself not the least indisposed to believe himself destined by the Divine providence "either in my own person or the persons of my descendants — to the possible enjoyment of health, wealth, and all manner of outward prosperity, in the evolution of a final natural order for man on the earth, or the development of a united race-personality." But when he is invited to regard the natural destiny of the race as adequate satisfaction to men's faith, he pronounced it "inexpressibly revolting. For after all is said that can be said, it is a mere reduction to order of man's natural or constitutional life, with the spiritual, functional, or infinite side of his being left out. And are men content to deem themselves cattle, that they expect

no higher boon at the hands of the DIVINE NATURAL
HUMANITY but an unexampled provision for their board
and lodging?"

What is needed is not primarily some further legislation, some reordering of our government or even our
economic system. Given the social spirit, these changes
will come of themselves. But the essence of the matter
is not in them. The essence of the matter is the full
consciousness on my part that *vir* is nothing apart from
homo; that I live only in my race, and consequently *will*
to surrender myself to my fellows, and lose myself in the
Lord. For James, any other than a religious way of putting this seemed inadequate and false. This faith he
could utter only by myth and by dialectic — and even
by rhetoric and satire. What matter, if we adumbrate
a religion which shall be democratic, a democracy truly
religious?

FATHER TAYLOR, or, METAPHOR AMONG THE METHODISTS

The Reverend Edward Taylor (1793–1871), for over forty years pastor of the Seamen's Bethel, Boston, was a Methodist saint. His warmth and wit drew local intellectuals and visiting celebrities to a church built for the edification of sailors on shore leave.

Not an educated man, he published no books, nor even sermons — indeed wrote none. The Spirit moved him to characteristic modes of oral teaching — in metaphor, in repartee, in polemic, in anecdote. He trusted the Holy Spirit that in the hour of utterance it should be given him what he should speak — and he spoke without guile or guard: he spoke the truth in love. He was a Son of the Resurrection, full of joy in the Lord.

Taylor had no dignity merely professional — not that of a man speaking honestly to other men. Dramatic and commanding, he did not require — what he could so effectively use — a provided setting. Like a proper saint, he was an unpredictable mixture of the practical and the unworldly: wise as a serpent and harmless as a dove.

Though Boston's long pride, Taylor was by birth a Virginian. In Richmond, as a boy, he used to preach funeral sermons over dead chickens and kittens — his auditors whatever Negro children he could assemble. When his rhetoric failed to move the 'mourners,' he whipped them till tears flowed adequately.

At seven, when he was picking up chips of wood for his foster-mother, a passing sea-captain asked him whether he wouldn't like to go to sea. His response was as immediate and complete as that of some whom Jesus called to be His disciples. He left his chips; and, without returning home to explain, followed the stranger.

At seventeen, a bronzed, handsome sailor went ashore at Boston. He stopped at Park Street Church; then, feeling out of place, climbed through a window into the nearby Methodist Chapel, where, under the preaching of Elijah Hedding, he was converted and became, with the demonstrativeness of his nature, a "shouting Methodist."

Though he longed to preach, even the Methodists, modest in their educational standards, could not accept a youth so nearly illiterate; so he went to sea again, embarking in a privateer. The crew were captured by a British man-of-war and presently confined in Dartmoor Prison. Here, at the wish of his fellow-mariners, he took over the duties of chaplain earlier performed by an Anglican clergyman.

The war over, Taylor came back to Boston, and instinctively, steadily, moved toward his proper goal and calling. He worked for a time as a peddler of tin and ironware and as a buyer of rags for a Boston junk-store. Presently, an old and devout widow of Saugus offered him a home in exchange for his looking after her farm. He accepted, and she taught him to read — though he continued to be read to while he listened, from the verse of Scripture which "spoke to his condition" and from which, in consequence, he could preach at one or another of the country schoolhouses.

In 1819, the presiding elder appointed Taylor to the seaport of Marblehead, and Taylor married a Marblehead woman, Deborah Millett, whose sense and sensibility both matched and complemented her husband's. Even more of her character than his appears in the anecdote of their wedding.

Absent-mindedly, looking twenty miles across Massachusetts Bay from Hingham to Marblehead, and consumed in the longing for the day of union, Taylor suddenly remembered — too late for making the journey — that this was itself the long awaited day. But his lapse made no difference. A day or two after, Deborah married Edward Taylor for time and eternity. In the course of her marriage, she became, 'in her own right,' not only "The Rev. Mrs. Taylor" but "Mother Taylor."

In their dealings with the mariner-preacher, the Methodist elders showed sense comparable to his wife's. They appointed the sailor to seaport circuits — among them, villages on the Cape and on Martha's Vineyard. At thirty-five, he was brought to Boston to be captain of the Seamen's Bethel — a church built and supported chiefly by Unitarian merchants — in order that he might proclaim the Methodist gospel to mariners unapproachable by essays on the 'dignity of man'; and Taylor's elders and bishops let him spread out his sails to the wind.

METAPHOR AMONG THE METHODISTS

Like Melville's Father Mapple, for whom Taylor was a chief archetype, Taylor preached from a marine pulpit. Behind it was a Protestant *reredos* — a large painting representing a ship in a stiff breeze — with ominous clouds visible above the masthead, their ominousness relieved by the emergence of an angel with extended arms and a golden anchor speeding on its way from heaven.

As the congregation gathered, Taylor paced his 'quarterdeck,' intent on seeing that only sailors were seated in the pews in the center of the Bethel, directly before him, while citizens from up-town, and distinguished visitors like Dickens and Harriet Martineau and Jenny Lind, were relegated to the side aisles and gallery.

"There he is, Bill," said a sailor one Sunday. "There's the old man walking the deck: he's got his guns double-shotted too; he'll give it to us, right and left. See how fast he travels — fifteen knots on a taut bowline. When he walks that way, he's well stirred up and ready for action." And stirred up for action he was.

He began one sermon by announcing, " 'Praise the Lord,' that's my text: it's somewhere between these two covers. I can't tell you exactly where; but that's it, so hold on to it. 'Praise the Lord.' " Ambitiously, he divided his subject into eleven heads; but the second got him into the deep waters of metaphysical argument. Suddenly he realized his peril. He raised his hand, and called out in a tone of command: "Hard down the helm! Hard down, the Helm! I've lost my reckoning — we're in the region of icebergs!" He turned. "I think I know my way yet. I'm going to make for the nearest port. I meant to have swept you round through other seas. But there's no time now; our miserable drift among the bergs has used up our voyage. Ah, I'm a poor captain, and careless; wonder I hadn't wrecked you! But it's not too late; and I'll bring you safe into port yet . . . "

If his texts were not always marine, his metaphors — at least at the Bethel — never stayed for long on land. St. Peter, he said, "was the last end of a thunderstorm, softened by the breath of the Almighty."

One Sunday, he attempted to convey the glad tidings of redemption. He described a terrific storm at sea. The ship sprang a leak, and then began to fill with water, and to sink, "deeper, deeper, *deeper, deeper.*" Suddenly the preacher looked toward the farthest end of the church. He cried out with piercing exultation, "A life-boat, a life-boat!" Most of the sailors sprang to their feet. Father Taylor extended his arms, and in a deep voice said, "*Christ is that Life-Boat!*"

Taylor was not always at the Bethel. He turned up at Methodist camp-meetings and preachers' conferences; took part in campaigns against rum — as well as against bigotry; made three trips to Europe, the last of them as chaplain of a ship carrying relief for the starving poor of Ireland, who were vastly charmed by his eloquence, wit, and blarney.

He was, whatever the setting, unpredictable: tender, sarcastic; witty, tear-drawing; polemic, oecumenical. He gave full utterance to every spontaneous half-truth, trusting that he would be moved to say the other half tomorrow, or, still more, that the whole truth — God's truth "spoken in love" — could take care of itself.

On a memorable occasion, when clergy of all Protestant faiths were seated behind him in the pulpit at Quincy, he denounced the heresy each — to his mind — represented; and when one of *his* sailors had submitted to Baptist immersion, saying that he "felt he must go down into Jordan," the old man, who knew the water in the Baptist tank was heated, said, "with a consuming sneer, 'Into Jordan? *biled* Jordan.' " Yet when, at a camp meeting, some dour brother rose to exclude from salvation all Catholics and Unitarians, all men who smoked and all women who wore jewelry, Taylor shouted out, "If that is true, Christ's mission was a failure. It's a pity He came."

He consorted intimately with the Catholic priests of Boston and their Bishop, Dr. Fitzgerald, at one ecclesiastical pole; at the other, he cherished some who had found even the Unitarianism of Dr. Channing a constriction.

To his Unitarian friend Dr. Bartol, minister of the West Church and the last survivor of Emersonianism, he said that Transcendentalism is "like a gull — long wings, lean body, poor feathers, and miserable meat"; yet the two men loved each other, and after the Methodist's death Bartol preached from II Kings 2:12, Elisha's touching words uttered as the mantle of Elijah fell upon him — "my father, my father."

Even Emerson came within his arms of loving-kindness. When, upon Emerson's resignation from the Second Church, Taylor heard the malicious rumor of insanity, he declared: "Mr. Emerson might think this or that, but he is more like Jesus Christ than any one I have ever known. I have seen him where his religion was tested, and it bore the test."

There was a puzzle, of course: no more than the elder Henry James could Taylor reconcile Emerson's life with his thought. But not being a metaphysician, Taylor could simply express both judgments without the need of synthesis. Emerson is "the sweetest soul God ever made; but he knows no more of theology than Balaam's ass did of Hebrew grammar. — If the Devil got him, he would never know what to do with him. There seems to me to be a screw loose somewhere, but I could never tell where; for, listen as close as I might, I could never hear any jar in the machinery."

Like the 'metaphysical poets,' Taylor thought in metaphors; and, like them, he did not disdain what Addison thought low forms of wit — especially punning. Here — and here alone — he touches Cotton Mather. At the prayer-meetings which ended the long Bethel Sundays, he especially indulged himself, sometimes in tropes, oftener — since he could not bear to be bored — in puns.

"See," he said, "the amber that is thrown on the shore, look at the pearls that come from the ocean — jewels fit to adorn the Saviour's diadem when he shall *ride over the sea* to judge the earth."

But, at the end of the long day, his wit grew more 'metaphysical.' When a wealthy merchant reminded the sailors of what the wealthy merchants of Boston had done for them and how grateful they should be, Taylor inquired: "Is there any other old sinner from up in the town who would like to say a word before we go on with the meeting?" A brother, saved, but slow in speech, was encouraged by the ejaculation, "Lubricate, Lord, lubricate." When the daughter of his friend Mr. Pigeon came forward for prayers, Taylor cried out, "Lord, sweep every squab off the roost." A Mr. Snow, tepid in his testimony, evoked "O Lord, melt that snow." The ardent speech of a Negro was greeted with "There is rain in that cloud."

The cause of retired preachers roused him to truly Oriental tropes. "They were moral giants, when God made them He rolled up His sleeves to the armpits. They are like camels bearing precious spices, and browsing on bitter herbs. They deserved to be carried on beds of down, their horses should be fed on golden oats, and they on preserved diamonds."

From 1861 to 1871 — especially after Mother Taylor's death, two years before his own — Taylor gradually failed, in a fashion not unlike that of his friend Emerson. Like Emerson, he failed in memory — but not in character, in conviction, or in courtesy. He did not recognize the Methodist bishop who paid a call upon him, but — after his wont — greeted his guest with the archaically Christian 'kiss of peace.' From the mourning coach, on the way to his wife's funeral, he bowed with Southern grace to unidentified poor Irishwomen. Over and over, he recited stanzas from the favorite hymns of his youth:

> Blest Saviour, what delicious fare!
> How sweet Thy entertainments are!
> Never did angels taste above
> Redeeming grace and dying love.

Ten days before his death he passed by the mirror, unable to recognize the tottering old man there reflected. But he made the stranger an exquisite bow, and then sought to convert him. Later, when the same image reappeared, he sang:

> Happy, if with my latest breath
> I may but gasp His name;
> Preach Him to all, and cry in death
> Behold, behold the Lamb!

It was observed — especially by his sailor 'sons' — that he "went out with the tide." He had often and eloquently expressed the desire that his corpse should be committed to the sea — a desire not fulfilled, since

Mother Taylor was already buried in Mount Hope. But the many funeral eulogies, not only at the Bethel but elsewhere, made partial amends. At the Pilgrim seaport of Plymouth, for example, the pastor preached from the 'happily' chosen text: "And when they had taken up the anchors, they committed themselves to the sea, and loosed the rudder, hoisted the mainsail to the wind" (Acts 27:40).

For two days, Taylor's body lay in state at the Bethel. All sorts and conditions passed by it reverently, among them Catholic women and children who, kneeling by the coffin, prayed for the repose of their dead friend's soul. At his funeral, held on Good Friday, distinguished clergy eulogized the silent preacher; but an old Irish vendor, unmindful of Protestant ways, walked into the Bethel with her basket of oranges on her arm, passed up the center aisle to the coffin, gazed tenderly at the face of the departed, and walked out.

Who were the New England saints? The Puritans, who, in their puritan days, believed a true church to be composed only of the elect, called themselves — as they were, derisively, called by others — the "saints." But their system did not work: long before Edwards' grandfather Stoddard, the 'Pope of the Connecticut Valley,' there were 'half-way covenants' or compromises; and when Massachusetts Congregationalism became divided between Unitarians and Trinitarians, the result of distinguishing the *church* (made up of communicants) from the *parish* (made up of respectable but 'unconverted' humanists) was palpable: in the region dominated by Boston and Harvard, the *parishes*, outvoting the *churches*, got possession of the old meeting-houses; and the 'orthodox' had to withdraw as 'schismatics.'

This much for the experiment of a church restricted to "saints."

Yet New England has produced saints — Christians of all persuasions. They would include, certainly, Edwards, the Calvinist; the first Catholic prelate of Boston, Bishop Cheverus; the Unitarian unwilling to be called a Unitarian whose spirit still dominates *New England* Unitarianism — Dr. Channing; the Anglican Bishop of Massachusetts, Phillips Brooks; the Swedenborgian missionary from Springfield, Massachusetts, born Chapman and known in American mythology (which has no saint save him) as Johnny Appleseed; the Methodist, Father Taylor.

A preacher, an evangelical actor, a poet in prose, Taylor was most of all a man of sanctified love. St. Augustine says, "the holy Magdalen changed her object only, not her passion" — a maxim deeply true of all saints.

Donne and Walton, believers in the Divine authorship of the Scriptures, yet both comment on the stylistic differences between the sundry *amanuenses* used by the Holy Spirit. Dr. Donne comments on the characteristic metaphors of those prophets who had been shepherds and those called from other vocations. Walton distinguishes between the idiom of St. Paul, with his rabbinical logic and high-flown eloquence, and that of the Saviour's most intimate disciples, who were called from their fishing to become fishers of men.

But we must also distinguish anglers from those who go down to the sea in ships, who can say: "All Thy waves and billows have gone over me, O Lord," and "Out of the depths have I cried unto Thee, O Lord." Melville properly gives Father Mapple the Book of Jonah as his text.

Father Taylor was not an angler, but a mariner. Converted, he remained an irascible and tender Virginian, alike characteristic in his scathing rebukes and his embraces of love and kisses of peace. Witty and eloquent, he did not abjure his gifts, but made use of them in the service of his Captain, who alone can kill the white whale and alone can give the tempest-tossed an anchor plumbing this oceanic life and alone bring them at last into the heavenly harbor and haven where "there shall be no more sea."

His literary contemporaries, even when clergymen, thought of Father Taylor less as a saint than as a powerful, uneducated, orator-poet. They were, after the fashion of Coleridge and Emerson, devoted readers of Browne and Jeremy Taylor, the Caroline preacher who died as Anglican Bishop of Down and Connor. Thus, when, in "The Problem," Emerson puzzles over his unwillingness to remain a priest, he invokes, as his most attractive Levite, Jeremy Taylor, who, as poet-preacher, combined two great glories of Eastern and Western Christendom — St. John Chrysostom and St. Augustine. The Anglican Bishop was "Taylor, the Shakespeare of divines."

According to his biographer, the Reverend Gilbert Haven, Father Taylor "read voraciously and luxuriated in" the work of his great namesake. But none of those who compared one Taylor with another supposed a debt: they clearly, and rightly, intended a parallel — in character, doctrinal position and, most of all, in style, for the Bishop, like Father Taylor, thought in tropes.

During his prime, Taylor was the only preacher of his kind in Boston — not merely because he was a mariner and a Methodist. To his left, there were the Unitarian clergy, cultivated essayists affirming the dignity of man; to his right, the Edwardean Calvinists, close, scholastic reasoners, affirming the Divine Sovereignty. Thinking in metaphors and parables, Father Taylor preached the reality of man's sin and the reality of God's Redemption, freely offered to all who, penitent, would accept their Saviour's love.

C. E. NORTON, APOSTLE TO THE GENTILES

"They who made England, Italy, or Greece venerable in the imagination, did so by sticking fast where they were, like an axis of the earth. In manly hours we feel that duty is our place." By practicing this their doctrine, Emerson and Thoreau and the Alcotts made of Concord our one shrine for literary pilgrims, native and European; nor can one doubt that the present civic well-being of that delectable town owes, in chief measure, to the examples of responsible citizenship set it by its intellectuals of the last century.

Today, with a few honorable exceptions, the village preacher and the village teacher endure rustication only till they can manage a "call" to the city; the literary man is restless till he can leave the provinces for New York and the cocktail parties of benevolent editors and publishers.

APOSTLE TO THE GENTILES

It was not always so. Mrs. Stowe's *Oldtown Folks*, a picture and interpretation of New England at the end of the eighteenth century, offers reliable witness. Through the pages of Sprague's *Annals of the American Pulpit* move, with the dignity of resolute purpose, the Calvinist clergy of New England, men of learning and intellect and civic zeal, ordinarily settled over a single parish for a lifetime and acquiring, thereby, the character as well as the style of parson, the person pre-eminent of the village. Hopkins of Newport, Bellamy of Bethlehem, Emmons of Franklin, Osgood of Medford: these parsons cannot be mentioned without invoking the parishes over which they were settled.

Even the New England factory village, when the owner of the "mill" still lived within its confines, could not totally escape from the feudal pattern. Seclude himself in hedge-fronted manor as he might, the man of wealth must drive past the tenements of the operatives; and sensibility if not conscience would compel a modicum of 'improvements' and relief. But where, today, are the admirable Lowells of Lowell and the Lawrences of Lawrence? Not, assuredly, in the depressing towns which bear their names. Of absentee directors and stockholders, the interest in factories can scarcely be other than abstract and financial.

Respectable government of our large cities is one of our despairs. Though their misgovernment is due to various causes, assuredly the chief remains, as Charles Eliot Norton saw in 1889, the fact that a "great portion of their inhabitants are but temporary residents in them . . . The sense in the individual of responsibility for the good of the community is weakened by the constant shifting and alteration of its members. A man naturally takes less interest in the affairs that concern the welfare of comparative strangers than in those which affect his friends; and naturally cares less for the welfare of a community of which he is a mere transient member than of one to which he is bound for life, and with whose past and future he is united by indissoluble ties." When men own no land, when they move from city to city with the restlessness or purely private hope of the contemporary American factory "hand" or clerk or salesman, how can they exemplify the civic honor for which the names of Athens, Florence, Venice, Nuremberg, Bruges, and old Boston are memorable?

The virtues requisite to a sound civic life are loyalty and responsibility; and these two were the principles by which Charles Norton lived and which, subtly and resourcefully exemplified, made him, during the last forty years of his life, the pre-eminent friend, professor of culture, and chief citizen of Cambridge.

Norton was born, as he died, at Shady Hill, a gentleman's estate of fifty wooded acres, acquired by his somewhat stiff and neo-classical father, with the aid of a handsome dowry through marriage with a daughter of the merchant prince Samuel Eliot. Yet Charles Norton's was a patrimony of more than stocks and bonds. Blood — such as the New World could boast — and social position were his. His father occupied a theological chair at Harvard, and, save for President Quincy, was the only Cantabrigian who kept a carriage. His uncle, George Ticknor of Park Street, had been the protégé of Adams and Jefferson, had a more brilliant social career in Europe than any other American of his time, was the intimate of Metternich and the correspondent of Prince John of Saxony. His younger relatives, like his cousin President Eliot of Harvard, partially replaced the dignitaries of his youth.

From his early years, the obligations of position were, by example and precept, impressed upon him. Federalist Unitarianism could scarcely offer schooling in humility: men were not worms of the dust or miserable sinners. Yet the New England conscience remained. Once willing to be damned for the glory of God, it could still erect itself to moral worth as, by the quiet eloquence of William Ellery Channing, it was bidden to do. Though Pharisaic sloth might lie ahead as the outcome of Boston Unitarianism, in Norton's youth, vestigial power was still present. The salt of the earth still felt the obligation to add savor to the less privileged world of Methodists, Baptists, and Jacksonian Democrats. Not by faith — not even by intellect — were men to be saved, but by character; and men of position must, by their steady exertion of self-discipline, their constant self-improvement, give leadership to slacker spirits.

During his freshman year at Harvard, fifteen-year-old Charles Norton, suffering from trouble with his eyes, was sent to New York for treatment. His father's counsels, administered by letter, represent the regimen under which Norton was reared:

"It will be a new experience of life for you; — somewhat of an early trial of your principles . . . I have strong trust that it will be on the whole beneficial to your character. So far as it is a trial you must regard it as an appointment of God, and endeavor to improve it as such . . . Though you can read but little in New York, yet the time need not be lost even as regards *intellectual* improvement. It is important for one fond of reading to understand and feel that information is to be gathered from many other sources besides books. I think you have very good capacity for observing what you see and hear, that you keep your eyes open, and your attention awake; and you now have a good opportunity for exercising your faculties in this way . . . Above all consider the events of life as intended by God for your discipline, for the formation of our characters. In life much is to be suffered as well as to be enjoyed; but sufferings may be alleviated and made blessings by the qualities of character which they call into exercise . . . "

When, at twenty-one, Norton left Boston for a journey to India, his father wrote him to similar purport: "You leave behind you an unsullied reputation, and the belief among all who know you that you have more than common powers of serving others. These are not things to make one vain. On the contrary, their true tendency is to produce that deep sense of responsibility — of what we owe to God, to our friends, and to our fellow men — which is wholly inconsistent with presumption and vanity."

These counsels, not dissimilar to what other sound New Englanders were offering their children, made a lasting impression upon the mind of Norton. Pious and somewhat humorless though they were, they enunciated what was deepest in the New England character and the New England view: Life is not given us for amusement but for responsibility; advantages confer obligations.

Partly influenced by his friend Arthur Hugh Clough, whose sacrifice of an Oxford fellowship to honest doubt he respected, Norton gradually withdrew from his father's theism and became, somewhat to the scandal of his Cambridge and Boston friends, an avowed agnostic.

Toward Catholicism, his attitude — witness the early *Notes of Travel and Study in Italy* — was firmly hostile. He cordially commended such humanitarian fraternities as the Compagnia della Misericordia. He venerated the character of Fra Angelico. In his careful essay on the building of the Cathedral at Orvieto, he accepted the Ruskinian view of the Middle Ages as a period when artists worked, not for fame but for the glory of God and the edification of children and rustics; and he admitted that, though minor motives of civic pride and intercivic rivalry may have played a part, the cathedral building of the period, requiring the labor and sacrifice of successive generations, presupposed deep and constant emotion scarcely to be denied the name of religion. Yet even in the greatest medieval achievements, fear of hell seemed to him the basic motive; and the eschatology of Rome, like that of President Edwards, belonged, he thought, to a "perverted system of heathenism raised upon a professedly Christian foundation."

In modern Popery he saw little save tyranny and superstition. He could admit that the Church performed some civilizing of the Irish peasant propagating his kind in Massachusetts; he could see that, through the confessional, it kept these immigrants pecuniarily honest, and chaste. On the other hand, he thought it treason that the intellectuals and the well-bred should turn to Catholicism for prop and stay. In Rome, Norton several times heard the Apostle to the Genteel; and of Dr. (later Cardinal) Manning he records the judgment: "A wily and soft dialectician, an ascetic by nature, to whom morals are subordinate to religion, who will lie for the sake of salvation, and who would cheat a soul into Paradise if he could not get it in honestly."

Protestantism, both in the older and its renovated forms, he judged a complete failure — intellectually superseded by the progress of science and devoid of spiritual influence with which to combat materialism. Christian Science, "most vulgar and debasing of modern sects . . . ungrammatical, unpoetic, absurd to the last degree," repeated the superstition of the Catholic Church, while divested of its dignity; Mrs. Eddy, whom, in 1901, Norton characterized as "the most striking and ugliest figure in New England today," painfully reminded him that "not only a few but the vast mass of the people even in New England . . . [were still] living in the Middle Ages."

In middle life, Norton seems to have entertained — in the company of Comte and his English disciple, Frederick Harrison — the notion that, not breaking with the past but abandoning dogma and ecclesiasticism, the Church might be transformed into an institution expressive of men's free loyalties and aspirations, society spiritually articulate. But the Positivist Church has gone the way of other attempts to put new wine into old bottles.

His paper on "The Church and Religion," however, set forth, eloquently, that view of 'true religion' which remained permanently his. It is, he defined, the "utter, absolute devotion — to whatever men know and feel to be best. It exists whenever the individual has learned that he has no private ends — that for all he is, and all he desires, and all he does, he is responsible to the community of which he forms a part, and which endows him with its united powers — that possession conveys no absolute right to property, but that every man holds whatever he possesses, be it genius, faculties, opportunities, or lands and goods, not as owner, but as trustee — and that the true worship of God consists in the service of His children, and devotion to the common interests of men."

With approving interest, Norton read the agnostic apologies of his friend Leslie Stephen; and to the end he regarded Christianity as offering selfish motives for good conduct, as a system of rewards and penalties, debasing to the intelligence and the dignity of human nature. Sometimes, to be sure, he feared that emancipation from belief in the supernatural might come so rapidly as to leave the masses unprovided with other inducements to right living: he was unoffendedly comprehensive of the alarm entertained at his scepticism, when his appointment to the faculty was under consideration, by some trustees of Harvard College; but habitually he trusted that, through moral education in home and school, and through the appeal to men's best selves, there should emerge a humanistic civilization built upon self-knowledge, self-control, grateful and intelligent recollection of the past, concern for the state, responsibility to the neighbor, loyalty to loyalty.

In later life, he was alarmed to observe the decrease of intellectual honesty on the part of the upper classes. In his own circle, Norton was almost the only avowed agnostic. Though in England, there were more, for the most part, the intellectuals, timorous for themselves or for the moral state of a faithless society, combined personal scepticism with outward regard for traditional beliefs. His friend Lowell, who felt incapable of reconciling the claims of the head and the heart, Darwinism and Christianity, retreated to the soft comforts of sentiment.

Much to Norton's credit, he did not play with Catholic modernism or with pragmatic defenses of religion or, in the manner of some eighteenth-century *philosophes*, endeavor to retain the authority of religion as, though mendacious, useful discipline for women, children, and the unlettered. To him such tactics would, properly, have seemed at once dishonest and fatal to the character of those pursuing them.

No distinction between the 'pure' and the 'practical' reason, between truth and expediency, will save civilization. To pragmatic suggestions that religion is true because it works, clear-sighted apologists will reply: no; it works because it is true. The whole moral effectiveness of religion, prized by some humanists, depends upon its being believed metaphysically or ultimately true, and, as such, defensible by trained intellects. As for the man on the street, about whose virtue the moralist is concerned, he has never yielded to philosophies of "as if" or "myths" or what nineteenth-century Germans — and Matthew Arnold — called *Aberglaube*. If he remains policed by religion, it is because he believes in a God above him and a moral government of the universe which is not the creation of his own conscience but objectively real.

It must be said, however, that Norton shared the Victorian illusion of supposing Christian morality, including its sexual prescriptions and prohibitions, to be severable from Christian faith. Like the 'radical' Emerson, he rejected the belief in which he had been reared without departing from its accompanying moral code; and — like Arnold and George Eliot and the other virtuous pagans whose positivistic ethics, examined by W. H. Mallock in *Is Life Worth Living?* and by Lord Balfour in *The Foundations of Belief*, are proved unfounded — he seems, rather naïvely, to have identified Christian morality with some universal code, discoverable by 'natural' reason and corroborable by human experience.

For this lapse the reason may be that, though primarily a moralist, Norton had no real acquaintance with the great ethical philosophers of the past and was quite unconcerned to define the principles or the bases of his own ethical thought. One does not doubt that other moral systems than those of Aquinas or Calvin can be devised, or that other *mores* than those which obtain in Anglo-

Saxon countries can provide cultural coherence and motives for action; the weakness of the Victorians lay rather
in supposing traditional English morality self-sustaining.

Another naïveté of Norton's is the antithesis between
popular religion and high morality. Just comparisons
must be made at the same level. The religion of the
masses may be reducible to a motivation of rewards and
threats; but the religion of the saints, whether Calvinist
or Catholic, may not so be defined. Dr. Samuel Hopkins'
test of Christian love was the willingness to be damned
for the glory of God; Edwards and Fénelon preached
and practiced "disinterested benevolence." If the saints
be few, so are the high Socratic ethicists. Common morality is maintained by fear of the police, fear of losing
one's job, fear of what other people will say, faith that
honesty is the most profitable policy.

For a New Englander, Norton was surprisingly ab-
stemious of self-analysis: indeed, he censored introspec-
tion as morbid. Nowhere in his writings does one find
those laments for lost faith to which Arnold and Clough,
in their poetry, were addicted. Nowhere, like Amiel,
does he brood and probe. For all his personal elegance
and his air of dilettantism, his collected objects of *virtù*,
and his occasionally patronizing utterances, he was a
man of action, a public servant. He had lost the Puritan
faith, to be sure; but he kept the sense of vocation.

There were times, of course, when self-culture attracted him, when the congenial society of England and
the history and arts of Italy made him desire the exile of
Story and James and Whistler. He looked back affectionately to the Federalist New England, believed that
"the very pleasantest little oasis of space and time was
that of New England from about the beginning of the
century to about 1825"; but with the commercial pros-

perity and "progress" which began after the Civil War and was still in full career at his death he felt no sympathy, and of its boasted achievements he was persistently critical. He frankly avowed that, for his own pleasure, he would have chosen to make Italy, or still more England, where he had found a congenial society, his home. What returned him to America and what kept him back was his sense of responsibility: to his children, who must not be deracinated, to his self-confident country, which stood in need of such loving and unsparing criticism as his own. As, in 1857, he wrote his friend, Professor Child of Harvard: "The grandeur of our opportunities is proportionate to the immensity of our deficiencies — so that one may rejoice to be an American even while seeing how far we fall short in many ways of what is accomplished elsewhere, and how much we have to do to make life what it ought to be and might be. But to be contented here one must work."

Norton worked. Though he was sometimes inclined to believe self-cultivation the chief service an American could render his country, and though his personal distinction was such as to justify his existence, he did not offer himself to his country as a mere example: he bent his efforts and his influence toward the accomplishment of whatever labor of civic usefulness was presented by others or occurred to his own projective brain. In collaboration with Lowell, but himself doing most, he edited the most solid of our quarterlies, *The North American Review;* he founded the Archeological Institute of America; he translated the *Divina Commedia* and the *Vita Nuova;* he inaugurated the Cambridge Dante Society. More than any other individual, he was responsible for the inception of *The Nation*, and for the eminently sound selection of E. L. Godkin as its editor. Late in life, he produced the "Heart of Oak" series of common-school readers, designed to acquaint the young American with "the intellectual life of the race to which he belongs."

The work eminently his was begun at the late age of forty-eight, when, at his cousin Eliot's appointment, Norton became the first Professor of the History of Art at Harvard and its first university teacher in the United States. For this work, all that he was, and all that he had learned, had prepared him; and the strength of his lectures came from their being the expression of the whole man. Tardy in his own aesthetic development, not himself a painter or in any other mode an artist, and always more conscious of the arts as aids to 'culture' than as aesthetic, Norton was nonetheless admirably equipped for his office. He had lived, not merely traveled, in Italy; and, without uncritical discipleship, he had profited from the enthusiastic guidance of his intimate, John Ruskin; he had pursued patient researches into the medieval records of Orvieto, Venice, Siena, Florence, St. Denis, and Chartres, making himself an exact scholar in what chiefly concerned him — the intellectual, political, and moral conditions under which such artistic achievements as building of cathedrals occur. As their friend, he was familiar with the personalities, the temperament, the methods, and the aims of many living artists, notably Morris and Burne-Jones; and, like Ruskin, a follower and purchasing patron of contemporary art as well as a student and exegete of the Italian primitives, he felt, and was able to make others feel, as a mere museum curator could not, the continuity between the past and the present. Lastly, believing in art as the expression of civilization and inseparable from the moral and political state of that civilization, he could present, to practical young Americans, a defense of the arts such as to recommend them to all who desired for themselves, and for their nation, the development of a balanced and complete humanity.

Norton's eldest son once aptly characterized his father's courses as "Lectures on Modern Morals as Illustrated by the Art of the Ancients." The integrity of the teacher's mind made any other course impossible. *Ut praesentia ditaret praeterita scrutabatur.* The real, as distinct from historic, judgments formed by a mature man must all proceed from the same center: Eliot could not apply one set of standards to the Periclean Greeks and another to the students at Harvard. The aim of the lectures was, of course, to present and to illustrate and to enforce the importance of civilization; and to this end Norton plied his learning, his wit, his sarcasm, his pathos, his character, till two hundred men, many of whom had elected the course as a palpable 'snap,' were shamed and exhorted into consciousness of our national shortcomings and into wholesome resolves to make their country venerable. In the judgment of John Jay Chapman, whose estimate has authority, this teacher had a more widespread influence on the students than had any other Harvard professor of the time.

After his retirement, in 1898, Norton continued to follow the development of Harvard, the increase in numbers and the expansion of the curriculum in American universities, and the altered standards of higher education and scholarship. He saw clearly the direction in which the colleges were moving: the opening of the curriculum to vocational skills, the increase of specialization, the dominance of German *Wissenschaft*, the overwhelming importance assigned to professional athletics. Before President Eliot had dragooned it into efficiency and science, Harvard had been a fraternity of scholars and gentlemen like Chil Lowell, Longfellow, and Goodwin: men to whom 1. branch of learning was completely alien; who possessed a common culture. But by 1899 this older world of humanists had passed away; and Norton, whose conception of education belonged, with whatever enlargements or corrections in detail, to the earlier and sounder order, could write: "Not even in Cambridge can I now get together half a dozen men or women round a table, who have a large common background for their thoughts, their wit, their humor. Literature in the best sense used to supply a good deal of it, but does so no longer. My fair neighbor asks, 'What are Pericles?' " Not compensatory for ignorance of the important was knowledge of the unimportant. Confronted with a statement of faculty researches and publications at the University of Pennsylvania, Norton was unimpressed to learn that one scholar had been compiling all the references to seasickness in Greek and Latin literature, and that another was continuing his investigations of the knee-jerk.

He was prompt to recognize and generous in his praise of academic performances which met his standards. For him, W. P. Ker's *The Dark Ages* and *Essays on Medieval Literature* placed their author with Mackail in "that union of culture with learning, of good letters with good scholarship, which is the boast of the best English scholars . . . and which is seldom shared by the Germans, who are apt to be nothing but learned, or by the French, who are apt to subordinate learning to pleasant easy literary style." Gilbert Murray and S. H. Butcher won similar commendation; and, among American scholars, Norton singled out George Woodberry, Irving Babbitt, Paul Elmer More, and George Santayana.

The same judicial temper, the same self-consistence,

marked his literary estimates — chiefly to be found in his letters. He read, without shift of standards, both the old and the new. An apparently instinctive *nil admirari*, kept in practice by a lifelong study of Dante, held to proportion his judgments of contemporary literature, even when it was the work of his close friends. He was slightly repelled by the "temperament of a tenor singer" in Byron, and by the *préciosité* of Pater; he preferred Malory to Tennyson's *Idylls;* justly defined Longfellow's talent as that of "saying beautiful things at the level of the broad public." *Leaves of Grass* he analyzed with equal absence of prudery and abandon: "Whitman has read the 'Dial' and [Emerson's] 'Nature,' and combines the characteristics of a Concord philosopher with those of a New York fireman. There is little original thought but much original expression in it. There are some passages of most vigorous and vivid writing, some superbly graphic description, great stretches of imagination — and then passages of intolerable coarseness — not gross and licentious, but simply disgustingly coarse." To a twentieth-century reader, "intolerable" and "disgustingly" are extravagant, but "coarse" and not "licentious" is the right distinction. The censure which Norton omits and which needs to be added is of Whitman's frequent sheer verbosity; but, with this emendation, the estimate can stand; and, written at a time when Emerson saluted his disciple, and Whittier committed his presentation copy to the parlor stove, it shows extraordinary discrimination.

A yet more exacting test-case was Emerson, for his sinless character and his angelic presence made estimate seem ungracious. Never was rebel so serene, radical so hallowed; and during his latter years, he enjoyed, in consequence, an apotheosis. Matthew Arnold's lecture on the "friend of those who would live in the spirit," delivered with temerity before the best Bostonians, evoked, by its preliminary distinctions, discriminations, and qualifications, the "provincial ire of the pure disciples." Yet Norton called it "a piece of large, liberal, genuine criticism," and quarelled with no part of it.

Norton's judgments of Emerson, frequent in his letters and his essays, are indeed clear-sighted and just, both in their discernment of the angel's rank among our authors and in their analysis of his position and influence. "No best man with us has done more to influence the nation than Emerson," he wrote in 1870; "but the country has in a sense outgrown him. He was the friend and helper of its youth; but for the difficulties and struggles of its manhood we need the wisdom of the reflective and rational understanding, not that of the intuitional. Emerson . . . belongs to the pure and innocent age of the Presidency of Monroe or John Quincy Adams — to the time when Plancus was Consul — to the day of Cacciaguida . . ." In 1883, Norton judged Emerson "nearer to being a poet than any other American . . ." Admirable alike for its boldness and its reserve, the judgment will command more general consent now than when it was written.

Returning from England with Emerson in 1873, Norton was impressed with the intellectual limits of his friend. "His optimistic philosophy had hardened into a creed . . . and, though of a nobler type than the common American conceit of the pre-eminent excellence of American things as they are, had hardly less of the quality of fatalism . . . Such inveterate and persistent optimism . . . is dangerous doctrine for a people. It degenerates into fatalistic indifference to moral considerations, and to personal responsibilities; it is at the root of much of the irrational sentimentalism in our American politics." Emerson had preached self-reliance; and men had been pleased to dispense with self-discipline and to trust to their temperamental selves; he had preached spiritual optimism, and Americans had grown confident that a *manifest destiny* was theirs and that, whatever they did, glory would attend the nation's future. The innocents abroad, the jingoists at home; Mrs. Eddy, who defined evil as an illusion of mortal mind and whose followers went about serenely, blandly smiling, and the New Thoughtists who identified religion with "success": could not all find texts in Emerson?

Perhaps our people had once been too colonial, too deferential to European opinion; but, Norton felt sure, the case was no longer so. What if our intellectual declaration of independence meant, not the production, at home and for home consumption, of great minds and great literature, but a mere national vanity which pronounced Peck the Pindar of Arkansas; which found an inglorious Milton in every village; which, in its journals, performed the weekly canonization of mediocrity?

The rapidity of our material expansion — the opening up of state after state, till from Atlantic to Pacific the land was occupied by men of energy and ambition; the accelerating increase in our population; the wonders of railroad, gas, electricity, speedily made available to the masses; in the world of 'culture,' the multiplication of public schools and public libraries: here were, indeed, achievements surpassing those of the Old World. The universe had never known our like before.

But what if, upon sober reflection — if, whirling across New York State to Chicago we had leisure for reflection — what if these conquests of matter and diffusions of comfort and literacy had produced no commensurate elevation or dignity? All men could read; but what did they read; all men could vote; for whom, so enfranchised, did they vote? In their rights to life, liberty, and the pursuit of happiness one may grant men's equality; but aesthetically, intellectually, morally, spiritually, men remain unequal.

Like Ruskin, Norton was a critic of society as well as of art; like Matthew Arnold, whose influence he deemed salutary, Norton offered his nation the faithful censures of a friend. Not to flatter his countrymen or praise them for their achievement was his office, but to expose their flabbiness and shabbiness, to shatter their idols, to warn them of imminent perils, to check their fatalistic self-confidence, to hold up to their emulation the complementary virtues of other nations — to be, in short, not their salesman but their monitor.

Like Arnold, Norton believed in political democracy; and he properly valued the spectacle of millions of Americans living "with more comfort, with less fear, than any such numbers elsewhere in any age have lived"; yet he knew that such a state is merely foundational to "civilization," and not to be mistaken for it.

Norton's social criticism began with *Considerations on Some Recent Social Theories* (1853), published when its author was twenty-six; and it continued till his death. From much said in his early book, Norton would later have dissented, though not from its prompting spirit. Distinctly, and youthfully, conservative, its tone cannot be called reactionary. The prefactory motto, apt for all Norton's criticism, comes from Edmund Burke: "Flattery corrupts both the receiver and the giver; and adulation is not of more service to the people than to kings"; in the spirit of the Old Whig, of Burke in his *Reflections*. the young critic counseled sanity, moderation, continuity, gradual change. Evils in the *ancien régime* assuredly there were; but rash reversals can effect no permanent good; and revolting against one error we may merely substitute its opposite. Untenable as the 'divine right of kings' doubtless is, the divine right of the majority is no improvement. It is not to the 'people' that we are to look for wisdom; their progress "must be stimulated and guided by the few who have been blessed with the opportunities and the rare genius fitting them to lead." The "recent theories" considered are those of such reformers as Kossuth, Mazzini, and Louis Blanc — the radicals of the day. The need of reform Norton does not doubt: European inequality in wealth is a reproach to civilization. But we must distinguish. Some inequality is correspondent to moral and intellectual disparities; some, the product of human institutions.

Not differentiating between these two kinds of inequality, Socialism proposes a Utopian state false to human nature. Again, sensitive to the abuses of private property, Socialism proposes to abolish its *use*, though, clearly, the responsibility inherent in ownership promotes the development of much which is best in character. Neither here nor later does Norton sufficiently analyze or develop his conceptions of just inequality and real property, nor indicate what checks should be imposed upon the growth of finance capitalism. Yet it seems evident that he was reaching toward such views as, under the name of Distributism, have, with Chesterton and Belloc, reached coherent formulation.

How, without rupture of the ties which bind us to the past, can we effect, gradually and peaceably, a more just state of society? Young Norton saw some hope in trade unions and yet more in co-operative associations; but he attached chief importance to the education of the poorer classes. "The first duty, the first necessity, is to help them to gain possession of their intellectual and moral natures . . . Education is the hope for the future of the laborer."

Between this early book and two essays, "The Intellectual Life of America" and "Some Aspects of Civilization in America" (published respectively in 1886 and 1896), Norton's thought underwent change both in essence and in emphasis. His book chiefly considered the state of Europe, where justice for the worker was the immediate necessity. In his essays, the most mature statements of his social attitude, Norton is addressing himself to the specifically American problem of democracy and culture, to the question, that is, "whether the highest results attained by the civilization of the past, and hitherto confined to a select and comparatively small body, can be preserved, diffused, and made the foundation of a social order in which all advantages shall be more equally shared; or whether the establishment of more democratic forms of society will involve a loss which such gains in human conditions as may result from the new system cannot make good, however much they may outweigh it in their sum."

In 1853, Norton still believed in religion, and could, when a problem seemed rationally insoluble, invoke the "will of God"; then, the republican form of government appeared feasible for America because of our widespread moral and intellectual training in the common schools and at home. But at the end of the century, religion — at least as commonly understood — had ceased to be an answer; the 'home' had relaxed its vigilance; and universal instruction in the rudiments of knowledge no longer offered assurance of responsible franchise.

Norton spoke out plainly: "The foreign boss of Tammany Hall, who rules the city of New York, who has assumed the garb of civilization and sits at rich men's feasts, is still a semibarbarian. The free school has not educated him, nor the hordes of his tribal followers. Yet while he and his fellows sell justice, commit daily barratry, practise blackmail, and make a scoff and byword of law, the self-complacent American looks on and says, with an optimism which he flatters himself is the spirit of genuine patriotism: 'Oh, it will all come out all right. Free education is the safeguard of the Republic.' "

Like the social criticism of the English Victorians, these essays seem less retrospectic than prophetic: the abuses they stigmatize have grown more palpable, more flagrant. The problems of the Victorians are still ours; nor can it be said that we have any solutions for them not found, essentially, in Ruskin, Newman, Pater, and Arnold.

Norton's survey of America is one painfully familiar: an advance in comfort and science, accompanied by a decline of fame, rank, learning, and honor as motives to action; the increasing reduction of power to a single species — wealth; the sensationalism of the popular press; the monotonous uniformity of our cities and citizens; subconscious conformity and moral timorousness; the prevalence of quantity over quality; the impudence of our children; the professionalization of university football and the abandonment of university Greek; the corruption of our politics; the deterioration of Congress; the steady growth of disrespect for rightful authority; the confusion of prosperity with righteousness.

It is a delusion, the aging Norton saw, to suppose the common school adequate to banish ignorance and to make our people capable of self-government. Yet for him, as for Arnold, education remained the only possible answer to modern and American ills. We have our minority, our "saving remnant"; and upon the proper education, aesthetic, moral, and intellectual, of the elect must be based such hopes for the future of democracy as a patriotic but cool-headed man can cherish. Said Norton, in the voice of Arnold: "The general tendency of modern civilization to render mediocrity the ascendant power in society has received no check, but seems, rather to become steadily more positive, and is exhibited on the largest scale in America." We have given a smattering to all, with the consequence, one might add, of giving to all an unwarranted self-confidence. But in seeking to educate the masses, we have neglected the chief task of a democracy — provision for the disciplines of full, rich, mature minds capable of leadership.

To be sure, public education cannot produce the genius; nor does anyone deny that an occasional great man is our sheer gratuity. Lincoln, of whom Norton's letters show him to have had a growing appreciation, might seem to show the futility of formal training. But Norton's clarity of vision was not blurred by the exception. The real value of education lies in its provision for a continuity of informed and responsible leadership — such leadership as is furnished by the English civil service and diplomatic corps, by Cantabrigians and Oxonians, men of trained intelligence and disciplined character, loyal to the civilization of the past and conscious trustees for the future.

Upon our universities, especially upon such of them as by their antiquity and endowments are independent of immediate pressure from alumni, the legislature, and 'popular opinion' upon the 'higher education' as such universities represent it, Norton would place his chief hope of our national well-being. But by 'higher' he did not mean more professional or more specialized.

"I call a complete and generous education that which fits a man to perform justly, skilfully, and magnanimously all the offices, both private and public, of peace and war," said Milton. The 'higher' education, in Milton's sense or Norton's, would not train the intellect or the memory alone, producing the specialist but leaving the personality unguided or perverted; the 'higher' is the more 'liberal'; and a liberal education, as Norton was careful to define it, not only ministers to the reason and the understanding but "quickens and disciplines the imagination, and, instilling into the soul of youth the sense of proportion between the things of the spirit and the things of sense, animates it with ambitions that are safeguards of character not less than motives of action . . ."

The burden thus placed upon the university is, alas, prodigious. Without assistance from traditional religion, without help from the deliquescing home, without an ethical system coherently articulated and systematically defended, the 'higher education' must, unaided, train, in taste and intellect and character, the elect minority committed to its care. And how will this minority of philosopher-kings effect the salvation of the state?

Like Irving Babbitt, Norton refused to commit his hopes to organization or lobbying or the enactment of legislation, or an army. Ultimately, he held, society can be improved "only, by the slow processes of self-government gradually embodied in public opinion"; only through the personal influence of the man who has himself achieved rectitude.

Whether, unaided, the university can sustain civilization one may well doubt; and, here in America, at least in our overgrown cities, one must question whether the personal influence of the *integri vitae* can sufficiently make itself felt to control a population emancipated from respect for its real as well as its nominal superiors. Norton's final ditch was Roman and Stoic. We must contend for what we believe right, though without assurance that it will prevail.

Civilization as we understand it may fail; let us, at least, not fail it. Norton was a Florentine, an Athenian, the upright aristocrat of a city state, the squire of Shady Hill. His own devotion to the *res publicae;* his loyalty to his principles; his self-consistency: these gave his career the hortatory force of example. No thoughtful American can turn to his *Letters* without being sobered and steadied; they constitute a civic education.

Norton was a gentleman: one of the purest examples we have produced. The true gentleman lives in the recollection that he is not "self-made," that all he is he owes; humility is not easy for those who "rise." Inheritance, to the gentleman, must be a perpetual trusteeship: what he has received, he must transmit; and, if he is faithful, he will leave to his children and his friends and the community in which he is incorporated an increase — not of specious but of real wealth, of culture, of character, of influence.

Sometimes the gentleman is an artist, like Henry James; sometimes a thinker, like Bishop Berkeley; sometimes a saint, like Fénelon. More often, he belongs in none of these supreme categories. To have real, though lower, value he need be no more than the morally responsible, intellectually responsive *honnête homme,* the protector and interpreter of the artist, the thinker, and the saint — the transmitter of culture, the guardian of society.

141

Such a gentleman, if I read him aright, was Norton. In his thinking, he stopped at the first wind, was inadequately persistent. For his character, he was far more indebted than he knew to the religion which he rejected.

IRVING BABBITT

Where is truth to be sought: in the old and time-tested, or in the new and unventured? In the intuitions of the individual or in man's corporate aspirations? Do we 'descend to meet,' or rise to standards socially set or sanctioned? Opposing ecclesiastical and all other authoritarian sanctions, Irving Babbitt always called himself an individualist and a 'positivist'; but such, in their current senses, were so remote that there seems a perversity in his very appropriation of the terms.

Transcendentalism, our earlier spiritual movement among New England intellectuals, had decried the institutional and the corporative and the conventional. Its men, 'disciples of the newness,' expected light to break next morning through the mediation of some child or crank. In their insistence upon the present and immediate utterance of God, they assuredly underestimated the value of tradition, even in religion and ethics.

Babbitt's mind took early its permanent stance. When in his twenties his closest friend, Paul More, came to know him, he had already become the integrated and inflexible person he remained.

His early stance was not the consequence of his coming — like Paul More and T. S. Eliot — from the Middle West to New England. Though he was born in Dayton, Ohio, and attended high school in Cincinnati, devoting a postgraduate year to the study of chemistry and civil engineering, he was not by temperament and certainly still less by conviction sensitive to his regional environment.

When he entered Harvard at the ripe age of twenty, both "over-prepared," by his own estimate, and sure of what he wanted and what he believed, he owed this clarity and determination to having a father against whom, violently, he could react. The easy formula is that Babbitt became whatever his father was not. It is too easy, but it carries one a distance.

Dr. Edwin Babbitt, a physician with a mind open at both ends, was a kind of naïve and belated Transcendentalist, forever moving from place to place and, upon failure after failure, incurably sanguine in the belief in the 'natural goodness of man' and in his own mission. At one period, he founded and made himself Dean of a 'College of the Finer Forces'; and he was a prolific writer of what are now called 'self-help' books — books covering everything from sex and color vibrations to faith healing and comparative religion, accompanying all his volumes, which he vended by mail, with copious charts and diagrams. Wherever he lived, he attracted cranks and crackpots of volubility and volatility approaching his

own. Dr. Babbitt was a hazy thinker and facile writer —
a kind of New Thoughtist of the variety current at the
end of the last century and far from extinct today.
Happily, Professor William James seems not to have encountered his writings, and probably even if he had he
— the laudator of Benjamin Paul Blood and Anne Payson
Call (author of *Power Through Repose*) — would not
have been able, in his tolerance, to take in one so vague
and eclectic.

In view of the temperamental and intellectual hiatus
between father and son, I end up by surprise that Irving
Babbitt's revolt against his father was not more total.
The son did not, after all, become either a Jesuit or a
stockbroker. If he thought, obviously, that his father
was a charlatan, he did not — as one of his favorite figures has it — "throw out the baby with the bath water."
He retained always a qualified respect for Emerson,
arch-hierophant of Transcendentalism; meanwhile he
went to work on two corrective lines — the first, to master, as a scholar as well as thinker, the Oriental thought,
Hindu and Buddhist and Confucian, so dear in its way
to the Transcendentalists and their deteriorate progeny;
the other, to equip himself with Hellenic culture, literary
and philosophical. Significantly, unlike his Hindu and
Platonic-drawn friend Paul More, Babbitt centered on
the least 'romantic' and 'mystical' ancients — on Aristotle and Sophocles, on Cicero and Horace.

He did his undergraduate work chiefly in the classics;
and after graduating from Harvard, in 1889, he taught
Greek and Latin for two years in the College of Mon-
tana. It was his desire to teach the Ancients as his permanent professional — and professorial — center; but he
was unable to sell himself to the classical scholars of Harvard. About prevailing methods of teaching Greek and

Latin he had no illusions. Their practitioners impressed him as chiefly antiquarians and curators, the dead burying the dead. But, believing the interment premature, he proposed to reanimate the sacred dead. When his services as resurrector remained unwanted, he turned, somewhat reluctantly, to French, the literature which he thought, after the Greek, most possessed of human wisdom; yet he never relinquished his attachment to the Ancients. Though he chiefly read during the academic year whatever current books and magazines would provide fresh illustrations for the "eternal laws written in the heavens," during the summer, until the very last, he turned back to his permanent sources of refreshment — Homer, Pindar, Sophocles, Horace.

Like Edmund Burke, Babbitt judged the bulwarks of civilization to be the spirit of the gentleman and the spirit of religion; his highest types of human endeavor were the *honnête homme* and the saint. In his college years he had studied Dante under Charles Eliot Norton, who, like Ruskin and Babbitt himself, refused to judge art without reference to the moral context from which it arose and the moral effects it subserved. He frequented Norton's Thursday evening *conversaziones*. Norton's portrait hung in his study. When, in later life, he made references to the 'gentleman,' he certainly did not forget one known.

Norton, in turn, was prompt to recognize his young friend's distinction of mind; and in the last year of his life he sent a friend Babbitt's first book, *Literature and the American College*, with an accompanying letter commending the author's "wide reading and independent thought." Babbitt's "conclusions are in the main such as you and I should approve . . . It is a great misfortune for us nationally that the tradition of culture is so weak and so limited. In this respect the advantage of England is great. But I hail such a book as Mr. Babbitt's as an indication of a possible turn in the tide of which another sign is the literary essays of Mr. Paul More . . ."

In his classroom, Babbitt was an experience not before encountered nor ever to be forgotten. Whether he sat or moved, he gave the sense of alert energy. The massive head was shrewdly lined. The piercing eyes and sardonic mouth effectually contradicted grey hair and stoop of shoulders. About him there was nothing genteel. A green bag, stuffed and bulging, accompanied his precipitate entrance; its contents — books and disorderly papers — were hastily discharged.

The 'lecture' offered no clerical or professorial firstlies and thirdlies — indeed had no discernible sequence, but, instead, a torrent of enunciations, theses, antitheses, and epigrams. Frequently the discourse would be interrupted by the mendacious announcement, "I choose an illustration at random" — as though the chaos of the desk could, unbidden, disgorge a suitable specimen. It did. The example, extracted from Wordsworth or from Mencken, or jaggedly sheared from a current newspaper or magazine, proved deliciously, laughably, apposite.

The Harvard *Catalogue* allocated Babbitt to the Department of Romance Languages; and indeed his examples often came from French, the literature in which he was presumably a specialist. But the quotations, even if first uttered in American French, were immediately translated, like the Latin in Burton's *Anatomy*, as though the point lay in 'message' not style; and quotations — innumerable in the course of an hour — came indifferently from English and American, German or Italian, Latin and Greek — now and then from Chinese or Pali or Sanskrit. They might be extracts from poets or other literary men, but they were almost as likely to come from historians, philosophers, theologians.

The puzzling and beautiful thing was the familiarity with which Babbitt invoked these great names. Their handsome and shelf-filling sets did not, as such, entitle them to any deference. In Babbitt's classroom, all authors and thinkers met as rigorous a scrutiny as though they had just been published. Said Emerson, when he was young but unabashed, "Meek young men grow up in libraries, believing it their duty to accept the views which Cicero, which Locke, which Bacon, have given; forgetful that Cicero, Locke, and Bacon were only young men in libraries when they wrote those books." Babbitt honored the illustrious dead by treating them as alive.

These books, 'works,' sets, all harbored blood. Men's emotions and convictions had gone into them and continued to course through the world. There was a battle of the books going on now — and always. Archaic heresies cyclically awoke; the error of yesterday became the novelty, the 'new thought,' of today. But the comfort was that the orthodox of former ages encompassed us and our contemporaries, encompassed us about as so many witnesses and guardians. Athanasius — or Irving Babbitt — was not really, whatever appearances might allege, a solitary champion, *contra mundum*, of the truth. They stood alone in their moment, perhaps; but against the aberrations of the moment we were to oppose the great tradition of which these isolated figures were the local representatives.

Babbitt, as, leoninely restless, he crouched at his desk, was ready, it seemed, to spring — was addressing his blows, thrusts, thumps at some unseen assailant, some enemy menacing the walls of the state, and — more

ominous — threatening the disruption of civilization.
What this adversary might be remained for a time uncertain; and when its name was disclosed as Romanticism
not every student's confusion remained unabated. He
could not, however, doubt that the enemy was real and
ominous; was certain that Babbitt saw, and grateful for
his vigilance.

Here was a new kind of teacher: not reducible to a
learned expositor, he taught with authority.

To Babbitt and his 'philosophy,' as one came to discern
it, one must have possessed the lethargy of a graduate
student to remain indifferent. He and it divided the class
into the receivers and the deniers; and upon the former
group his influence was unquestionably hypnotic. That
sanity should cast a spell, that counsels of restraint, de-
cency, and moderation should grow enticing — surely
that was paradox. Yet so it was.

Babbitt indoctrinated the faithful; of that there can be
no doubt. By many of his students, his orthodox formu-
las were parroted, his favorite quotations repeated. Such
practice is immature, of course; yet for this superficial
imitation of the master, Harvard could furnish sufficient
and equally egregious parallels — not alone in Kittredge.
Since the many will ever imitate naïvely and with inadequate flexibility, it becomes a choice between their models; for men's normal growth in virtue and wisdom
comes from the imitations of their heroes: their history
is that of their friendships and their admirations. The
method has its perils; but surely so feeble an 'originality'
as not to survive discipleship scarcely deserves preserva-
tion.

It is history that Babbitt's abler students passed beyond
docility to a more creative imitation. Without ceasing

to feel or to avow their debt, they learned to distinguish between the essential and the peripheral or 'personal' in what was taught them. Babbitt felt genuine and unassuageable pain at the defection of every disciple: he was frequently more sensitive to differences than to agreements. One must concede, however, that his power over other men proceeded from precisely this unwavering conviction that he saw the truth. To see him as *self*-assertive was to misread him. Assertive of convictions, he had no more interest in himself as a 'person' than in the 'personalities' of others. He never grew autobiographical, either in lectures or books; and if he denounced self-expression as the highest aim for the raw it was not in order to make exception for himself.

It was in the name of Truth that he was grieved by deflection. To his distress that his old friend, Mr. More, and his younger friends, like Mr. Sherman, should have fallen into error, he gave honest and incautious avowal. *Amicus Platonis, sed magis veritatis amicus.* Against Van Wyck Brooks, who has publicly witnessed his high respect for Babbitt, against Mumford and Lippman and Santayana, whose *Life of Reason* might deceive, if possible, the very elect into thinking it a more subtle version of Babbitt's 'Humanism,' and against T. S. Eliot, his former student, he protested, even though to looser minds all those spirits might appear, in their several ways, defenders of the true cause.

Possessed of more detachment, he might well have said to his lapsed disciples, "When me you fly, I am the wings." For Babbitt's service as teacher transcended his doctrine. If to some who knew him only through his books he doubtless seemed an obscurantist, for his students he was primarily an enlightener and an enlarger.

Under his tutelage they first grasped the possibility of a literary history which should be more than names, facts, isolated authors, or beautiful passages; comprehended the interpenetration of literary and social life; were compelled to define their terms, articulate and defend their principles. Babbitt taught men to think; and if those whom he inducted into this discipline came to differ from him, it was he who gave them the standards by which they found his doctrine at this point or that defective, his practice imperfect. T. S. Eliot has typically testified: "Having myself begun as a disciple of Mr. Babbitt, I feel that I have rejected nothing that seems to me positive in his teaching."

Babbitt's closest profession was the academic. He was not ashamed of being a teacher; and his chief service, it may well be, was performed within Harvard College and within the American university. At a time when eminent professors were eminent for their ability in the practice and direction of research, Babbitt, almost alone, sought to develop the critical spirit and the critical method. His hostility to the American doctorate, conceived and administered according to nineteenth-century German patterns, was caused by no distaste for learning, at which, for range and depth, he was the peer of his ablest colleagues, but from the conviction that the university should be, pre-eminently, the institutional embodiment of the critical spirit.

Though, for a brief moment of unfortunate publicity, Babbitt became identified by New Yorkers with a cause which bore the undefinable name *humanism*, it was recognized in the academic world that he was also the proponent of a cause in one sense larger and more catholic — the cause of the humane study and teaching of literature. At Harvard he fought, in behalf of every Ameri-

can professor who believes that his function compre-
hends interpretation and criticism, against all who would
restrict the academic office to fact-finding, fact-compi-
lation, fact-reporting. If, to doctrinal 'liberals,' he was
patently reactionary, he defended an academic freedom
precious and perishable — the freedom to judge.

I have spoken of Babbitt's influence in the University;
yet — a commanding, invigorating, illuminating teacher
— Babbitt seemed in no sense academic; and it was not
only unjust but grotesque when his journalistic adver-
saries sought to belittle him by affixing the pejorative
Professor or Doctor — the latter a title he, like G. L.
Kittredge, had never won. A 'Professor' may be a man
who has collected, in his memory and in his 3 x 5 cards
and his filing cabinets, what has been said on both sides
of every question — a man who, though lacking much
mind or taste, has led so respectable a life that the university administration cannot indict him for 'lack of co-
operation,' moral looseness, or activity in local politics.
Babbitt's virtues were more vigorous and more positive.

Learned in many languages, he yet seemed a scholar
only in the mode of the seventeenth century, or, still
more, in the Emersonian sense: he was Man Thinking.
The amassing of facts as such never enticed him. He
was concerned with principles, with tracing lines of intellectual development.

He had not spent his days 'browsing,' as it used to be
called; had no such temperamental incapacity for decision as to necessitate whiling away his time by a dip into
whatever print lay handy. The library was not his her-
mitage but his arsenal.

For books as things in themselves — elaborate bindings
or rare editions — he had no particular taste. As a mat-

ter of fact, cheap texts served his purpose better, since his concern was with what was said. He turned the pages of books with moistened thumb and finger, dog-eared their corners, penciled them with heavy, blunt marks of dissent or approval, bulged their covers with clippings and notes and markers. The library in his house consisted chiefly of books used in his courses and of those presented to him by disciples and allies.

This unbookishness was a source of power to Babbitt. His mind and will dominated the more feminine and empathic virtues of critics like Lemaître. With the romantic virtues of 'wise passiveness,' sensibility, and subtlety he had, indeed, little sympathy. His was a masculine nature — vigorous, independent, forthright, dogmatic, and pugnacious — with an analogy, so obvious as to be platitudinously remarked, to Dr. Johnson's.

Aesthetically he was undeveloped and unconcerned. Art he judged almost exclusively by moral criteria; and its importance for him lay in the emotional persuasiveness which art could furnish to doctrine — doctrine, true or false.

Literary criticism in the strict sense Babbitt rarely practiced. He comes nearest it in his *Masters of Modern French Criticism* — a criticism of critics — and in certain essays, notably his introductions to college editions of Renan's *Souvenirs* and Racine's *Phèdre* (1902 and 1910). His *New Laokoön* exhibits him as a brilliant and penetrating excoriator of *mélange des genres* — of picturesque poetry, poetic pictures, prose poems, poetic prose, and literary ('program') music. But he lacked intimate acquaintance with painting and music; aesthetically he was unequal not only to Brownell and Santayana but to men so immeasurably his inferiors in critical stature as Huneker, Mencken, and Paul Rosenfeld.

Why, then, did he not become an avowed philosopher? Though Babbitt never, to my knowledge, articulated his reply, it can be inferred. Few read the works of philosophers; fewer yet comprehend them; and yet fewer are moved by them to change their way of life. Most men are impelled to action by philosophy only when their passions have — at least concomitantly — been aroused. Literature Babbitt conceived of as ethics "touched by emotion." Every novelist, dramatist, or poet has an attitude toward life determining the selection of his themes and orienting his whole book. Babbitt liked to quote with assent Napoleon's maxim, "Imagination rules the world"; and it followed, for him, that the critic's chief office is to 'try the spirits' which move men, to test the quantity and the quality of influence exerted by men of letters.

He was, in short, primarily a moralist. Metaphysics, as developed since Kant, he pronounced bankrupt. For him, as for his friend P. E. More, the Absolute was a mirage if not, indeed, a demon. He called himself an empiricist or a "positivist," and sought to refute Rousseau and Bacon, the types, for him, of emotional and utilitarian romanticism, by appeal not to theory but to their 'fruits' in conduct. The current "positivist" is a relativist; "but," affirmed Babbitt, "I am immediately conscious in myself of an abiding one as well as a changing many." Though the self-avowed 'empiricist' is likely to be some version of behaviorist, Babbitt affirmed the experience in himself not only of the passive, recipient, and perceptive but of an active principle of control, manifested most signally when, in the name of his 'higher will,' he disciplined his desires. If the empiricist would appeal to the experience of the race, then he must include the testimony of the sages and the saints in addition to that of the common man; he must include the experience of the Orient as well as the Occident.

In consequence of his emphasis on the *frein vital* and on the evils of most of what, from the late eighteenth century to our own day, has passed for 'progress,' Babbitt has passed for a Puritan and a constitutional denier. Like his admirer, the brilliant Wyndham Lewis, he has seemed most appropriately cast as the 'Enemy.' In hearty satire and invective he furnished the appropriate foil for his old and most influential assailant, Mr. Mencken.

Had Babbitt been placed in a 'classical' age, would he not have opposed its orthodoxy — was not his real role that of adversary? With his appeal to balance and symmetry, he would certainly have protested, as indeed he did in Cambridge, Mass., against formalism and pseudo-decorum; but that he would have been a rebel for rebellion's sake it is difficult to believe. His convictions, like Burke's and Johnson's, went deeper than what passes for common sense, or than what he himself called "humanism"; but he had no affection of novelty, no wish to be thought 'different' or 'original' — though, in the best sense, he was both. That he felt isolated seems palpable; but it is equally certain that, instead of feeling his solitude a comfort, he found it, so far as his sturdy nature could admit of complaint, a grievance.

In the once fashionable parlor pastime, he was asked, "When, in the past, would you like to have lived?" He did not hesitate to choose the Athens of Pericles. Yet he had no taste for putting such questions. He accepted the age and the locale into which Providence had placed him, thinking such matters no part of his choice or responsibility, and no 'environment' determinant of character.

His cosmopolitanism, markedly inclusive of the Orient as well as Europe, never made him less an American, and an American of mid-Western origin, born in 1865 and by profession a teacher at Cambridge, Mass. Of countries save his own, he loved France best; and his occasional sojourns there were perhaps the most happy periods of his life; but his attitude toward travel differed little from that of Emerson and Thoreau. It was the French mind, not the quaint and picturesque, with which he sought to acquaint himself; and he never visited India and China, despite his mastery of the Sanskrit and Pali tongues and his life-long study of Hindu, Buddhist, and Confucian thought.

His wife, reared in China, used, in the early years of her marriage, to rebuke him for professing to understand that country as she did not. "You have never been there," she would say, "you don't know how it looks and how it smells." The rebuke passed as superficial. To know the *mind* of China is to know its essence; and Babbitt, who had assimilated the Buddhist scriptures, knew far more about Java than his English brother-in-law, to whom the natives of that island, among whom he had long lived and worked, were a lot of dirty beggars.

Babbitt saw much that was shoddy and superficial, faulty and false, in America and his countrymen; and, in something of Arnold's spirit, though without Arnold's languid snobbery, he sought to supplement and rectify our national character. This involved no Anglophilism or Francophilism. Respecting the older, firmer civilizations, he was too sane to suppose that the benefits of those cultures could be acquired by the adoption of tweeds, tea, berets, or *vin rouge*. Like Emerson, he sought to develop, and to exemplify, a culture which, having sloughed off the provincial, should yet remain indigenous.

What will become of his books, most of them dictated to his wife in the pungent, racy, vigorous idiom of his lectures, it is difficult to predict. He was repetitious, after the fashion of professors; like Arnold and every other effective propagandist, he was topical in his illustrations. A time may come when Babbitt's remarkable books will no longer be read. But such a prospect would not have silenced him; his estimate of his literary powers was modest, and he lacked the last infirmity of noble minds. Honestly, honorably, persuasively, in unpropitious times and climes, he bore his witness.

There is no name properly inclusive of Babbitt's whole system. If the professor called it all "Humanism," he was practicing what Newman, in speaking of the Alexandrian Platonists, calls "economy" — adjustment to a context of time, place, and education.

No one can read Babbitt's later books attentively without feeling the schism in his doctrine: on the one hand, the adjuration to humanism as sensible, moderate, decent, and decorous; on the other, the exalted 'enthusiasm' with which he invokes the "higher imagination" and the "higher will."

It is my own judgment that Babbitt himself was not a 'humanist.' His familiar trichotomy divided attitudes toward life into the naturalistic, the humanistic, and the religious; and it has naturally been assumed — not without Babbitt's 'economy' — that, highly as he spoke of high religion, he was himself unable to transcend the second level. This, I think untrue.

A proper statement of Babbitt's position must be contextual. To be 'religious' in the West meant to be Christian — and, for Babbitt as for his disciples, almost all of them religious — Orthodox, Roman Catholic, or Anglican normally, less commonly orthodox Protestant (in the sense of Barth, Tillich, or Niebuhr); or it meant to be 'humanitarian' — a concept often, by the simple, identified with Babbitt's own 'humanism.'

Babbitt held orthodox Christianity in high respect — most of all, the Catholic Church. At Harvard, he taught for years a course in Pascal. He read with general sympathy the 'Catholic intellectuals' of our time, for example, Maritain and Gilson. He gave a kind of 'deathbed *imprimatur*' to L. J. A. Mercier's *Challenge of Humanism* (1933), which translates Babbitt's system and terms ("the higher will") into their Thomistic equivalents.

In his attitude toward Anglicanism there was, perhaps unavoidably, a mixture of contempt for so loose-thinking ("comprehensive," in its own term) and laxly-discipling a Church, with personal pain at the conversion to such a 'system' of three thinkers close to him — G. R. Elliott, T. S. Eliot, and Paul Elmer More: I arrange these names in what, for Babbitt, would have been an ascending order.

As for Protestantism, Babbitt experienced it in its 'liberal' and 'humanitarian' period — the period between the great President Edwards and his scarcely less great disciples — and the 'Crisis *Theology*' of today. To William James's Gifford Lectures he did injustice — though intelligible caricature — by calling them *Wild Religions I Have Known*. And he rejected James's 'pragmatism' — as he rejected its equivalent in 'Catholic Modernism' — the more vehemently, doubtless, because it might be mistaken as his own position. The pragmatist, he says, "does not conceive of truth as something that already exists: he makes his truth up as he goes along; in other words, he takes that to be true which seems useful or agreeable to his ordinary self."

Of older attempts at a monistic religion, Babbitt persistently repudiated Stoicism, not only for its monism but for its "pride"; and he was quick to discern and dissociate himself from all its modern versions, including his former student Walter Lippman's *Preface to Morals*.

No one, to my knowledge ever accused Babbitt of being a Buddhist, and, indeed, had any one done so, Babbitt would doubtless have denied the charge, understanding his prosecutor to be thinking in terms of 'revelation,' 'authority,' and sectarianism. Yet, according to his comprehension of pure Buddhist doctrine, Babbitt could have been — and, in my judgment, was — a Buddhist. Speak respectfully though he might of the Catholic Church and its "dogmatic and revealed" religion, Babbitt as personally and firmly rejected both 'dogma' and still more, 'organized' or 'institutional' religion — that is, the Church — as he rejected the Church's acceptance of a metaphysics, whether Thomistic or Augustinian. But in these rejections, as in his rejection of theism, he was perfectly in accord with what he calls "genuine Buddhism," the Hinayana Buddhism which survives in Ceylon and Burma.

In not avowing himself a Buddhist, Babbitt was doubtless partly motivated by not wanting to seem an eccentric — like, say, Dwight Goddard, who published a *Buddhist Bible* at Thetford, Vermont. Whoever heard of an "American" Buddhist? Yet he was centrally motivated, I think, by the desire to restate "genuine Buddhism" in modern terms, as a religion acceptable to those who, like himself, found metaphysics, theology, mythology, and ecclesiasticism harmful rather than salutary to the devout life.

Babbitt was acutely sensitive to the importance of terminology; yet his own attempt at creating a set of modern terms for his faith was scarcely successful — indeed scarcely intelligible. Some of these terms were taken over from modern thought — for example, "positive" and "experimental"; others were of his own devising — "the higher imagination," "the higher will." But by "positive" he did not intend the "positivism" of Comte, and by "experimental" did not mean to invoke the techniques of American laboratories. He best defines these terms in the essay "Buddha and the Occident," which, though written in 1927, was published only posthumously, accompanying his translation of the *Dhammapada*, as a memorial of what his widow called his "whole life's devotion to the study of Buddhism."

Religion in the Occident has come to seem "a mere matter of *dogma* and *tradition* in contrast with a point of view, the scientific, that is *positive* and *experimental*. It is here that the study of great Eastern teachers . . . may prove helpful. The comparative absence of *dogma* in the *humanism* of Confucius and the *religion* of Buddha can scarcely be regarded as an inferiority." *

Buddha "differs from the Western religious thinkers with whom we are familiar by his *positive* temper. The idea of experiment and the idea of the *supernatural* have come to seem to us mutually exclusive. Yet Buddha may perhaps be best defined as a *critical* and *experimental supernaturalist*." "Buddha may be defined indeed, in contradistinction to a *naturalistic empiricist* like Hume, as a *religious empiricist*."

* *The Dhammapada*, tr. by Babbitt (1936), 68, 78. The italics here and in subsequent quotations from Babbitt are mine.

IRVING BABBITT

Babbitt's distinction between the 'lower' and the 'higher' will is probably best expounded in his "Europe and Asia," a chapter of *Democracy and Leadership*. "In India . . . , the will to which man subordinates his ordinary self is often conceived, not as a divinity that transcends him, but as his own higher self." Beyond any other religious teacher, Buddha "plants himself on the naked psychological fact" of the opposition "between man's higher or ethical self and his *natural* self or expansive desires"; so that Buddhism, in its original form, is the most *critical*, or, if one prefer, the least mythological of religions."

Though primarily concerned with showing how close Babbitt's position came to that of the 'natural theology' ('natural' as distinct from 'revealed') of Scholasticism, Louis Mercier came near to understanding Babbitt's 'Buddhism.' He not only recognizes a "superhumanism" as well as a "humanism" in Babbitt's system, but remarks that the theory of the 'higher will' is "wholly original," "so peculiar to him that most of the discussion concerning his doctrine shows that it is not fully grasped . . ." — was not even grasped by Babbitt's closest friend and ally, P. E. More.

Comparing Babbitt's terms with those of Catholic Scholasticism, Mercier rightly glosses the "higher imagination" as "intellect" — that which apprehends universals — and as "imagination controlled by intellect and will"; while the "higher will" is the psychological equivalent of Christian 'Grace,' the study of which, for orthodox Christianity, belongs to revealed religion.

Babbitt, as a 'genuine Buddhist,' was metaphysically agnostic. To be sure, he "unhesitatingly" ranged himself "on the side of the supernaturalists" and — we may add — on the side of the superhumanists; but that commitment did not involve theism or a metaphysical settlement of the debate between 'determinism' (or Calvin's "preordination" and "inscrutable decrees") and 'free will.' To deny theism was, for him, "an inverted dogmatism," while to affirm it was to leave the realm of experience. The "final answer to all the doubts that torment the human heart is not some theory . . . but the man of character." Christ gave the Asiatic answer to Pilate's "What is truth?" by saying "I am the Way, the Truth, and the Life." But Christianity "transcends *positive observation* . . . in its tremendous projection of personality . . . into the region of the infinite and eternal." Life reveals its secret, Buddha seems to say, "only to the man who *acts*; and, of all forms of action, the most difficult is *inner action*."

Quoting from his translation of the *Dhammapada*, Babbitt adds: Buddha "has succeeded in compressing the wisdom of the ages into a sentence: 'To refrain from all evil, to achieve the good, to purify one's own heart: This is the teaching of the Awakened.' The Buddhist commentary is interesting: when you *repeat the words,* they seem to mean nothing; but when you try to put them into practice, you find they mean everything."

Babbitt was often accused of making the center of his spiritual life a veto — named "inner check," a phrase he had taken, by way of Emerson, from Colebrooke's *Essay on the Vedas.* But this 'check' — the will's equivalent to Socrates' 'daemon' uttering an intellectual 'No' — was, as Colebrooke's comment makes clear, not some ritual taboo but the name for the dualism between the 'lower will' and the 'higher': "He who eternally restrains . . . the earth, *the same is thy soul* and the Internal Check immortal." "The Internal Check is the Supreme Being." A relevant gloss on this passage would be the

162

Biblical text, God's words to man, "For my ways are not as your ways, neither my thoughts as your thoughts, saith the Lord."

That Occidentals have misunderstood the Buddhist doctrine of Nirvana is puzzling when one considers the limited and cautious statements concerning Heaven made by the Christ and St. Paul: "Eye hath not seen, ear hath not heard, the things which God hath prepared for them that love Him." But Babbitt understood. In reply to the common Western view that Nirvana is annihilation, Babbitt says: If one " 'dies' entirely to the natural self and its impulses, what follows — if we are to believe the great religious teachers — is *not mere emptiness but the peace which passeth understanding.*"

How Babbitt came by his Buddhism must remain a matter of conjecture. When he came from the Middle West to Harvard as an undergraduate, he was already a student of Buddhism; and when More first knew him, Babbitt was learning Pali, the language of the Buddhist scriptures, while More, drawn to Hinduism, was pursuing Sanskrit. Emerson is perhaps the most likely instigation: there is a real continuity between the Transcendentalist devotion to the 'Sacred Books of the East' and the 'Humanists' attachment to Eastern thought.

However he came by it, he made it his own. Despite an appearance so Yankee — so "Amurican" — he drew to him, at least in later life, Orientals in search of wisdom. In Paris, where — not long before his death — he lectured at the Sorbonne, he was visited by Chinese, Japanese, Koreans, Hindus. "These men," says an American witness, "came to him as to a great sage. Their every gesture and intonation suggested admiration and reverence . . . Babbitt was probably the only American of our time who was regarded by Orientals as a *wise man* in their own tradition and who knew exactly how to receive the homage of their discipleship."

After his friend's death, Paul More wrote of a Hindu who, having visited Harvard, came on to Princeton. For a moment, the Hindu's comment amazed More: "Oh, Babbitt — he is a holy man, a great saint!" Then More, reflecting on the distinction between Western and Eastern conceptions of sanctity, remembered that in the East "the Saint is a man notable rather for his *will-power* than for *meek submissiveness*"; and he understood.

As a professor and teacher, Babbitt generously practiced the 'humanistic' art of "meditation" the adjustment of standards to persons and occasions; but when, on his deathbed, his wife, invoking the name and habit of his friend More, urged that he divert himself with a detective story, he roused himself to give answer both Buddhist and Christian: "Good God, I can *meditate*."

JOHN BROOKS WHEELWRIGHT

Wheelwright was of Boston as Thoreau of Concord.
Bostonwise, though he knew his Europe — the Paris of
Hemingway and Fitzgerald — he had never traveled
farther west than Albany. But he had traveled much in
Boston — from the Somerset Club and the Hill to the
South End.

When, in 1940, a speeding truck killed this irreplace-
able American, his friends, who had taken for granted
that good old Jack would go on being his unpredictably
amusing, exciting self, were left with an unpredictable
sense that what was lost was not — now that time for
diagnosis had come — so peripheral: that he was a serious, meticulous poet; not a minor wit but a master of
metaphysical poetry.

For long, "Wheels" had been one of Boston's spectacular divertissements. He was the current representation of its wit and audacity — the apostolic successor to Mrs. Jack Gardner and Amy Lowell, Father Van Allen of the Anglo-Catholic Church of the Advent, and H. T. Parker, music critic for the *Transcript* and sole male resident of the Hotel Vêndome.

His lineage was symptomatic, symbolic. On his father's side he descended from the Reverend John Wheelwright, a Puritan who fled Laudian England, in 1636, only to encounter the stringencies of theocratic Massachusetts Bay. Though a Calvinist, he was a strong advocate for freedom of religious opinion, a zealous backer of the Antinomian Anne Hutchinson, who accused most of the clergy of teaching the Covenant of Works, not of Grace. In 1636–37, Wheelwright was the preacher at the Fast Day of the Boston Church; in consequence, Governor Winthrop and the General Court summoned him before them, pronounced him "guilty of sedition and contempt," and banished him and his friends from the Colony. It is he who is invoked in "Bread-Word-Giver" as ancestor of rebels and anarchists and reformers and other 'enthusiasts,' whom New England has never lacked — from Williams to Alcott and Garrison and the Adamses to Sacco and Vanzetti and Robert Lowell — and of whom "Wheels" claimed membership by birthright.

> Saint, whose name and business I bear with me;—
> rebel New England's rebel against dominion;
> who made bread-giving words for breadmakers;
> whose blood floods me with purgatorial fire;
> I, and my unliving son, adjure you:
> keep us alive with your ghostly disputation
> make our renunciation of dominion
> mark not the escape, but the permanent of rebellion.

JOHN BROOKS WHEELWRIGHT

On his mother's side, there was political power and wealth. John Brooks was Governor of Massachusetts from 1817 to 1822, six terms. His second cousin, Peter Chardon Brooks (1767–1849) built, through money from the East India trade, a mansion at Medford. At his death in 1849, he was reputed to be the richest man in New England. Brooks's estate in West Medford boasted what "Wheels" (which, as symbolically dialectical, he liked to term himself) calls in the note to "Paul and Virginia," "The most splendid garden of Massachusetts, where the author spent the summers of his early childhood."

The Brookses were not Jack's sole claim to grandeur. "Footsteps" is alleged — with what warrant I don't know — to be, in style, a continuation of "Alexander's Feast" by "the Author's seventeenth century kinsman, John Dryden." And in "Argument" (that is, notes) to the same volume, the last published and the most radical, the second stanza of "In Poets' Defense" is affirmed to take its origin from "an oration by that flower of New England [a choice specimen of double-talk, that phrase], the Author's mother's father's uncle by marriage, the Honorable Edward Everett."

Now forgotten, what prize didn't that "flower" once win? Graduating from Harvard with highest honors, Everett was installed as minister of the celebrated Brattle Street (Unitarian) Church in 1814, before he was twenty. In little more than a year, he was offered, and accepted, the newly founded chair of Greek at Harvard. To prepare himself, he took a Ph.D. at Göttingen, the first American to receive the degree. In 1819, he not only began his professorship at Harvard but became Editor of the solid, British-imitative *North American Review*.

Now it was the time for such a man to make a correct and profitable marriage; and in 1822 he wedded Charlotte, daughter of Peter Chardon Brooks.

A scholar, clergyman, professor, Everett was also an orator of elegance not before known in New England; and he had both charm and ambition. Backed by his father-in-law's money, he was in turn a member of Congress for five terms, Governor of Massachusetts for two terms, Ambassador to England (1841–45), and President of Harvard, 1846–49. The "flower of New England" indeed! The phrase becomes satirical when one thinks of how the first Wheelwright, and Roger Williams, and Alcott, and Garrison, and John Jay Chapman would — like Jack — have judged him. Even the charitable Emerson, after celebrating the learning and rich rhetoric of the young Everett, ends his eulogy by the quiet damnation: his work was "a triumph of Rhetoric. It was not the intellectual or the moral principles which he had to teach. When Massachusetts was full of his fame, it was not contended that he had thrown any truths into circulation."

Like all 'proper Bostonians,' Jack derived from the proper marriages of 'mind' on the one side and, on the other, money and social correctness. Both sides have their 'claims' and their rewards. Jack was duly aware of being, in his own person, both a 'gentleman' and also an Independent. But, clearly, it was the line of the 'Bread-Word-Giver' which, so far as he could, he chose. He first showed his rebellion by a series of adolescent pranks calculated to shock his own social class, Bostonly ruled by decorous women, and to the end of his days he felt it one of his duties to be an authorized shocker, a conscientious violator of all genteel refinements. To assure himself that he was being candid he had to surrender all fear of being taken for rude. If he liked, he took a nap on a park bench; forced his citizen's way into the Ritz or the Vêndome unclad in the ritual garments; at restaurants banged with knife and fork upon his table till the waiter had corrected an order carelessly heard or imperfectly prepared.

Since he followed no 'gainful occupation' and was able to construct his own calendar, he was free to pursue a whim or dilate upon a notion with leisure more characteristic of the speculative hobo than of Boston's dutifully busy 'leisure class.'

While relinquishing no single privilege of the adolescent aristocrat, he made, as he grew older, more significant revolutions, which the ritual pranks but symbolized. He rebelled against the ancestral caste-religious Unitarians, becoming an Anglo-Catholic, of a never very orthodox variety. He rebelled against capitalism, becoming a member of the Socialist Labor Party. An Anglican and a Communist, he took the minority and purist and perfectionist view of each allegiance; yet in both cases he endeavored to subordinate his marked individuality to society, the redeemed form of man.

His third rebellion was against verse merely refined and talented. He wanted a prophetic and menacing poetry. With Emerson, whom, as revolutionary and poet, he respected, he loathed the "tinkling of piano strings," would have the kingly bard "smite the chords rudely and hard." Taking the ancient and primitive view of the poet as the maker, seer, and sayer, he was impatient of less grandiose pretensions.

And Wheelwright was a poet, reared as a child on William Blake's *Songs* and in maturity never weary of arguing his theories of prosody. In 1931 he wrote his *History of the New England Poetry Club, 1915–31,* a privately printed account of a club still extant, which had Amy Lowell and Josephine Preston Peabody as rival candidates for the first presidency. After some aesthetic violence, the conservatives (under Miss Peabody) won out, despite Miss Lowell's feeling "that, were she not elected, poetic experiment would appear repudiated by her fellow New Englanders."

The *History* is so rich in gibes, purported naïvetés, and constant irony that I must abjure further quotation and but cite a few facts. Starting as a hoax on the activity of a humorless but verse-writing and reciting graduate student, the Harvard Poetry Society was founded in 1915 by E. E. Cummings, Foster Damon, John Dos Passos, Robert Hillyer, *et al.*, presently anthologized as *Eight Harvard Poets*, to be followed by *Eight More Harvard Poets* edited by Malcolm Cowley and Wheelwright, who of course included their own poems. The 'Harvard Poets' were soon annexed to the Boston group, largely female and 'refined.'

From 1928 till death, Jack was institutionally loyal to the New England Society, served as Vice-President and general minor official. Not in accord with the refined and conventional 'line' which prevailed to the production by the members of rondeaux and villanelles, he attended — not to murmur appreciative sighs but to bear his witness, offer his criticism of that which had been read, as seriously as though it had been a poem by Blake or Donne.

I do take seriously the opening sentence of the *History*: "It is impossible to write poetry which is merely poetry, or American poetry which is merely American. Poetry must be poetic in a particular way; ours must be American in a New England way." Not for him the Poetry Society of America: rather than that he would put up with his fellow-Bostonians, whom — difficult as they might be to take, personally or doctrinally — he regionally understood.

The 'causes' which engaged him were felt to be one cause. Jack was not a dialectician; and he could not, cerebrally or verbally, have synopsized Poetry, Catholicism, and Communism; but he held, by faith, that the *summa* of the future would properly adjust their parts and demonstrate their compatibility.

In the 'Argument' which followed his *Political Self-Portrait*, he wrote of his last book: "What will emerge is rather more humanist than materialist, and much less a political treatise than a self-portrait of one who has found no way of turning, with Scientific Socialism, from a mechanical to an organic view of life than to draw from moral mythology as well as from revolutionary myth . . . Just as the Church through Scholasticism once squared faith with reason, and just as already Christian Ethics have abandoned Divine Predestination for Economic Determinism, so religion (which is the social ethic of the imagination) must transform itself and dialectic materialism." And Poetry is, of course, the mode whereby the imagination is socially operative. "The main point is not what noise poetry makes, but how it makes you think and act, — not what you make of it, but what it makes of you."

The consequence of this theory and this life was four books of poems. The last (with a magnificent poem on Buddha) was ready for publication at his death, fifteen years ago; but his literary executor has, on one pretext and another, not seen fit to bring it out. If most of Wheelwright's friends found it difficult to assemble him for appraisal, they found it yet more difficult to appraise his writing. They took his books as the concomitants of taking him; and taking him was — if one cared for his ease — taking a high grade of intellectual excitement. Wheelwright's published books, *Rock and Shell, Mirrors of Venus,* and *Political Self-Portrait,* are, to a degree almost unparalleled, extensions of his total self, private as well as professional. There are the poem-by-poem dedications to his friends, his relatives, and occasionally his favorite enemies — poems not correlated to the dedicatees save as, by principle, one must bind one's personal and one's doctrinal loyalties. Trusting the reader to "bear in mind that it is impossible to say a poem over in prose," Wheelwright felt free to supply each volume with an "Argument," a copious and racy commentary upon the poems, in which he disserted (in a fashion neither Shavian nor Jamesian) upon matters bibliographical, autobiographical, ideological, and prosodic. These comments, far from prose paraphrases, should be taken before or after, not with, the poems.

There are the long 'mythic' poems: "Forty Days," "North Atlantic Passage," "Twilight," "The Other." These are Wheelwright's most recalcitrant work. He has indicated their sources in the Cabala and the Talmud, the Apocryphal Gospels, 'lost and hostile gospels,' the Nestorian Acts of the Apostles — testimonies to his zeal for the 'minority rights' even in Christian tradition. His inveterate Seth and Cain (in *Political Self-Portrait*) are, to be sure, investments of St. Augustine's *De Civitate Dei,* according to which these two sons of Adam are founders of the rival cities, mundane and spiritual, so that human history is the record of Cain's war with Seth. But even with these helps, they remain 'prophetic books' in need of careful exegesis before judgment can be passed.

Mirrors of Venus, a modern *In Memoriam,* was in

process of composition over a period of twenty years; and its general scheme is the poet's own movement, emotional as well as intellectual, from concern with the private self, its desire for private love and private happiness and private survival after death, to faith in the corporate solidarity of mankind, the Resurrection which is the transcendence of the 'personal.' But so to state it is to give the doctrine rather than the movement, which never reaches this solidarity. This too is an 'Ash Wednesday.' It is a flagellation of the introvert, carried out with a startling minimum of the rhetorical or elegiac; it is a determined effort to whip the sentimentalist's fine wonder at his own fine feelings.

Structurally, this effort means taking the most conventional of forms, the sonnet, the form consecrated to amatory sequences and hyperbolic compliment, and subjecting it to all manner of inversions and distortions, more radical than those of Dr. Merrill Moore. And these ingenuities — in one instance, the provision of three concurrent rhyme schemes — were intended to give writer and reader a tough, quasi-mathematical obstruction to any approach of the sentimental. In any case, it would be nearly impossible for a New Englander to have written with such central depth and candid innocence if he had not given his sequence the look of a scholastic construction. But the devices were more than protective mask: they were valiant and generally successful efforts to formalize self-pity and the like spreading and formless emotions.

The precise order in which the 'sonnets' are arranged could probably be altered without disaster to the continuity but the poems, individually ponderable, gain mass by consecutive reading, their total effect being that of a musical 'suite' in which there is a general counterpoint of moods, tones, and movements. The styles are extraordinarily varied: low-pitched and conversational, or playful, or grotesque; direct or oblique; imagistic or metaphysical; thin or densely crowded; elliptical or logical. There is the conversational mode of "Sophomore," in which the sentence falls amiably into the easy verse with the unemphatic disyllabic rhyme:

> When, catching his own glance, he analyzed
> what stared so impolitely from the mirror,
> he wondered if he earnestly despised
> that callow face; or did he hold it dearer
> because, unlike his classmates, he preferred
> talk with autumnal women, ever mellow,
> or boys, with whom his well-considered word
> not always marked him as a crazy fellow?

There are the playful, didactic wit of "Mother," and the imagism of "Week End Bid, I," and the *symbolism* of "Summer."

Wheelwright's obvious, difficult job was to sum up his parts; and at this he was but infrequently successful. The integers, such as "Father," survive repeated examination.

> An East Wind asperges Boston with Lynn's sulphurous
> brine.
> Under the bridge of turrets my father built, — from
> turning sign of *Chevrolet*, out-topping over gilt State
> House dome to burning sign of *Carter's Ink*, — drip
> multitudes of checker-board shadows. Inverted tur-
> reted
> reflections sleeting over axle-grease billows, through all
> directions cross-cut parliamentary gulls, who toss like
> gourds.
> Speak. Speak to me again, as fresh saddle leather
> (Speak; talk again) to a hunter smells of heather.

JOHN BROOKS WHEELWRIGHT

Come home. Wire a wire of warning without words.
Come home and talk to me again, my first friend.
  Father,
Come home, dead man, who made your mind my home.

The octave and the sextet are in counterpoint: the rest-lessly kinetic picture of Boston from the River, not im-ages alone but symbols of Church and State ("asperges," "parliamentary") and the Capitalism which out-tops the State; then the prevailingly monosyllabic and abruptly rhymed invocation, with its extraordinary simile, as remote as the felt distance between city scene and in-voked father; the undeterred bold repetition of simple words, the sloganlike alliteration (after the fashion of an advertisement or a neon sign), the sure emphasis of the last three nouns (man, mind, home): these make a poem continuously rewarding in detail and built into a whole by the precarious mode of a two-part movement without the aid of a repetitive and conclusive third.

From these bold variations from the sonnet, Wheel-wright turned to bolder experiment. Some of the poems in *Political Self-Portrait* are relics of early composition (their author was likely to keep pieces long by him, inviting and — when he assented — accepting the aid of those to whom, so eagerly, he read them aloud); but the characteristic new work, intractable to scansion either by stress or syllable, is yet scarcely to be mistaken for pre-Eliotic free verse. In contrast to the sonnets, it offers a public poetry, to be recited or chanted unself-consciously. Its claim to being poetry lies in its resource-fulness, its vivacity, its surprises.

Like all New Englanders, Wheelwright was a didactic poet; but he had learned some things from the mistakes of his elders: he does not carefully separate his picture from his moral or his song from his sermon; and one judges the earnestness of his propagandistic intent not by any pontifical tones but by his willingness to clown, to shout, to clatter, to repeat, to pun, to alliterate, to jingle — in order that the reader shall stop to listen and, stopping, not sleep. It was designed chiefly, I suppose, to show the 'workers' that poetry need not be academic or epicene. Critically, there is no harm in calling the consequence intellectual vaudeville, if one stress the adjective equally with the noun.

Like other revolutionary poets, Wheelwright found it hard to give poetic particularity to a series of future blueprints; but he knew, with precision, what made him squirm, and he had a brilliant talent, in life and in letters, for the satire which travels from its inception in a lampoon to its finale in the caricature of a class. It is not the hatred of what he once adored: the satire bangs away at the poet's old enemies — the smug, the complacent literati, the profiteers and the frauds.

But Wheelwright's concern for a revolution — his soapbox homilies in the South End of Boston, when, raccoon-coated and elegantly waistcoated, he would, like a 'penitent nobleman,' urge his listeners to do away with his Class, were never invitations to the proletariat to enjoy the delights of gadgetry. The theme of "Redemption" is a revolution which shall effect the union of Deed and Word, of Art and Christianity. In his note to the poem, he asks whether "future proletarian patronage of a public standard of sophisticated living . . . [may turn out to] be as half-hearted, almost, as present capitalist patronage?" and answers, "At any rate, one can never be premature in arousing the masses to their cultural duties and to the joy of living."

About his native city and region — for he was a regionalist whose flights to New York were brief — his feelings were equally ambivalent. "I don't hate the South," says Quentin of Mississippi to Canadian Shreve; and Jack's narratives of Boston's horrors and his indictments of the confused city — vulgar and refined — were of analogous order.

The feeling was always there: the love and devotion, the prophetic 'Woe unto you'; but they reach their most subtle power in "Come Over and Help Us," a poem — "written in Blake's seven beat epic meter" of the Prophetic Books, which is, says Wheelwright, "a rhapsody on the type Bostonian."

The title is the "Macedonian Call" (Acts 16:19) and is "addressed to the world that is not Boston."

Our masks are gauze/ and screen our faces for those
    unlike us only,
Who are easily deceived./Pierce through these masks to
    our unhidden tongues
And watch us scold,/scold with intellectual lust;/scold
Ourselves, our foes, our friends;/Europe, America,
    Boston; and all that is not
Boston:/till we reach a purity, fierce as the love of God;
    — Hate.
    . . . .
Madness, we so politely placate/as an every-day incon-
    venience
We shun in secret./Madness is sumptuous; Hate, ascetic.
    . . . .
We are not tireless;/distract us from thin ecstasy, that
    we may hate
If with less conviction,/with some result, some end, —
So pure ourselves; so clear our passion;/*pure, clear,
    alone.*

The New Englander leaves New England/to flaunt his
    drab person

Before Latin decors/and Asiatic back-drops.
Wearies./Returns to life, — life tried for a little while.
A poor sort of thing/(filling the stomach; emptying the bowels;
Bothering to speak to friends on the street;/filling the stomach again;
Dancing, drinking, whoring)/forms the tissue of this fabric, —
(Marriage; society; business; charity;—/Life, and life refused.)
The New Englander appraises sins,/finds them beyond his means,/and hoards.

Wheelwright had the New England conscience, the New England originality. There were predecessors whom he respected — Blake, Emerson, and Emily Dickinson; but he was constitutionally incapable of imitating or being schooled, and he sounds like no one else. He had to learn for himself and say for himself, eager for the criticism of his friends, unwearying at revision, but prophetically indocile. The outcome was a poetry uneven, often, by intense intension, gritty and gnarled, but rich, inclusive, felt as well as thought, symbolized not asserted, languaged in a New England vocabulary which, like Emerson's, is both transcendental and homely.

Wheelwright was a saint; he was also a poet whose books will one day take their rightful place in American poetry and scripture.

AUTHOR'S NOTE

I dedicate this New England hagiography to the memory of Irving and Dora Drew Babbitt and of John Brooks Wheelwright; and, with gratitude, to Norman Foerster and Warner Rice; and I wish it to serve as a thank-offering to New York University for my incumbency, in 1953–54, of the Berg Visiting Professorship of English and American literature.

The men of whom I here write, my spiritual ancestors and kinsmen, have occupied my thought for long, and I have written, and published, on some of them; but the sense of their continuity and common calling has come to me only recently — with the peace and joy of illumination.

Included in this book are closely revised, and often refined upon, versions of "Alcott, Orphic Sage" (*The Hibbert Journal*, April, 1931); "Emerson as Self-Therapist" (*Measure*, Autumn, 1951); Chapters VII and VIII of *The Elder Henry James* (New York, Macmillan, 1934: long out of print); "Charles Eliot Norton" (*The American Review*, November, 1936); "A Portrait of Irving Babbitt" (*The Commonweal*, June 26, 1936). To the editors and publishers of these earlier versions I owe gratitude for their permission to add, subtract, revise, and reprint.

THE SOURCES

For books available in early New England, cf. Thomas G. Wright, *Literary Culture in Early New England 1620–1730* (1920) and Chapter VI ("Libraries, Private and Public") of Samuel Eliot Morison's *The Puritan Pronaos* (1936).

Anne Bradstreet's *Works* are best edited by John H. Ellis (2d edition, 1932). The last stanza of her "Contemplations," which I quote, derives from Revelation 2:7: "To him that overcometh will I give . . . a white stone, and in the stone a new name written which no man knoweth save he that receiveth it."

The anagrammatic poems by the Rev. John Wilson, first Teacher of the First Church of Boston, were celebrated by the Rev. Cotton Mather (cf. *Handkerchiefs from Paul* . . . Edited by Kenneth B. Murdock [1927], p. liv). This mode of poem, in which the *name* is, as in the Scriptures, regarded as significant, was continued by others, notably the Rev. John Fiske (1608–77), Pastor of Salem, and author of an elegy on the Rev. John Cotton, whose name is anagrammatized as "O, Honie Knott." Fiske, hitherto unknown, was discovered and

181

interpreted by Harold Jantz ("The First Century of New England Verse," *Proceedings of the American Antiquarian Society,* Vol. LIII [1944]).

Modern editions of Wigglesworth's *Day of Doom* and of the first New England-born poet, Benjamin Tompson, have been edited respectively by Kenneth B. Murdock (Spiral Press, 1929) and by Howard J. Hall (*Benjamin Tompson ... His Poems,* 1924). Tompson's "The Grammarian's Funeral" is to be found in *American Broadside Verse: From Imprints of the Seventeenth and Eighteenth Centuries,* selected and edited by Ola E. Winslow (1930), pp. 24–25. Tompson thriftily used this poem twice, first for his predecessor as Master at the Boston Latin School, John Woodmancy, and much later as "Published upon the Death of the Venerable Mr. Ezeziel Chevers, the Late and Famous Schoolmaster of Boston in New England." Cheever died in his ninety-fourth year. Tompson, who followed Woodmancy and preceded the venerable Cheever at the Latin School, is buried in the old Roxbury graveyard under a slate stone bearing the impressive characterization, "Learned Schoolmaster, and Physician, and the Renowned Poet of N. Engl."

The Rev. Nicholas Noyes (b. 1647; B.A. Harvard, 1667, Minister of Salem, 1682–1717) is a Baroque poet — "the last and greatest of our Fantastics," Moses Tyler calls him (*A History of American Literature During the Colonial Period,* Vol. II [1878], pp. 38–43). Tyler quotes Noyes's punning but serious Elegy on the Rev. Joseph Green of Salem; Miss Winslow (*op. cit.,* p. 21) reproduces Noyes's verses addressed to the Rev. James Bayley of Roxbury, suffering from 'the stone,' a fertile conceit even when all the stones are Scriptural.

The verses by the Rev. Joseph Capen, Minister of Topsfield, on the death of Mr. John Foster, mathematician and printer, I quote from Rufus W. Griswold's *The Poets and Poetry of America* (16th edition, 1855), p. 17. The original broadside has disappeared; but the 'conceited' elegy has survived in various forms. Capen's conclusion elaborates Benjamin Woodbridge's ikon of John Cotton as a book which, in Heaven, will appear in a new edition purged of errata; and it may be supposed that the same figure, in Benjamin Franklin's self-epitaph, has a printer's lineage.

To the late Baroque poetry of the Rev. Edward Taylor

THE SOURCES

(1645–1729) I have given the opening essay of my *Rage for Order* (1948).

President Urian Oakes's "Elegy" upon the death of his close friend, the Rev. Thomas Shepard, Teacher of the church at Charlestown, is given in *The Puritans* (edited by Perry Miller and T. H. Johnson, 1938), pp. 641–50; Joshua Moody's epitaph for Lydia Bailey, in Jantz (*op. cit.*, p. 263).

For a brief history of metrical psalms, cf. Canon Adam Fox's *English Hymns and Hymn Writers* (1947), pp. 12–16, and, for the American succession, Hamilton C. MacDougall's *Early New England Psalmody . . . 1620–1820* (1940). Selections from the *Bay State Psalm Book* (*The Whole Booke of Psalms Faithfully Translated into English Metre*, 1640), and the Rev. Richard Mather's first draft of the Preface, expositing the translator's principles, are conveniently available in Miller and Johnson's *The Puritans*, pp. 555–60 and 669–72.

The Rev. Mather Byles I have written upon in "To Mr. Pope: Epistles from America," *P.M.L.A.*, XLVIII, pp. 61–73.

ORTHODOX PARSONS OF CHRIST'S CHURCH

This is not a theological essay but a modest tribute to the ethos of those eighteenth-century New England clergy who — right-wing Calvinists, as we might call them — were disciples of Jonathan Edwards. Like their teacher, they were scholars and systematic theologians, as well as educators, both of their clerical successors and of their generally rural or provincial congregations. Though, after the Puritan tradition, they married, they were clearly men who lived under spiritual and intellectual discipline: I would call them, as I evoke them, 'Protestant Scholastics.'

The Rev. W. B. Sprague's first two volumes of *Annals of the American Pulpit . . .* (1856) constitute a hagiography of the "Trinitarian [or Orthodox] Congregational" Clergy, in distinction from the "Unitarian Congregational." In New England, still, the former adjective defines the theological position; the second, the form of ecclesiastical organization.

Edwards A. Park of the Andover Seminary, one of the last of the Edwardean tradition, wrote not only a memoir of Dr. Hopkins, prefacing the *Works* of that theologian (Boston,

183

NEW ENGLAND SAINTS

1853) but a *Memoir of Nathanael Emmons* [the pastor of Franklin, Mass.]; *with Sketches of His Friends and* [theological] *Pupils* (Boston, 1861), a memoir running to 468 pages octavo: though big, never boring.

Mrs. Stowe is — in, and out of, her New England novels — a firsthand witness. Cf. her review of Sprague's *Annals*, "New England Ministers," the *Atlantic Monthly*, Feb., 1858; *Oldtown Folks* (Boston, 1869), especially Chapter XXXIV; and "Old Father Morris: A Sketch from Nature" (Vol. XIV of *The Writings of H. B. Stowe*, Riverside Edition, Boston). Mrs. Stowe excels the two excellent epistolary biographers of "Father Morris" (in "Nature," the Rev. Samuel Mills, Pastor of Torrington, Connecticut) by reproducing his sermons and sayings in "the strong provinciality of Yankee dialect."

Enoch Pond, the author of *Sketches of the Theological History of New England*, was one-time Professor at the Bangor Theological Seminary and, by his testimony, "became a Congregational minister of New England sixty-five years" before 1880, when he published his *Sketches*.

For Father Fisher, of Blue Hill, Maine, cf. Mary Ellen Chase's *Jonathan Fisher, Maine Parson, 1768–1847* (New York, 1948).

NEO-PLATONIC ALCOTT

The still standard life of Alcott is Frank Sanborn and W. T. Harris' *A. Bronson Alcott* (1893), though now supplemented by Odell Shepard's somewhat popularized *Pedlar's Progress* (1937) and his edition of the *Journals* of Alcott (1938).

Alcott's *Orphic Sayings* appeared in *The Dial*, Nos. 1 and 3 (July, 1840, and January, 1841). *Tablets* and *Table-Talk* (1868 and 1877) both contain a "Speculative" half. The third volume of Alcott's philosophical prose, *Concord Days* (1872), includes essays on Pythagoras, Plato, Plotinus, Boehme, Berkeley, and Coleridge.

Alcott's library of a thousand volumes, chiefly imported from England, contained almost the total repertory of the mystics: Thomas Taylor's translations of Plato, Plotinus, Porphyry,

THE SOURCES

Jamblicus, Proclus; the Cambridge Platonists; Sir Thomas Browne; the list was published in *The Dial* (Vol. III, pp. 545–48) and was reprinted in Clara Sears's *Bronson Alcott's Fruitlands* (1915).

As well as a Neo-Platonic philosopher, Alcott was a life-long educator. For the latter concern, cf. Elizabeth Peabody's *Record of Mr. Alcott's School* . . . (1835) and Alcott's *Conversations with Children on the Gospels* (1836–37), both accounts of the Temple School in Boston; the three remarkable printed reports of his superintendency of the Concord Public Schools, to be found in the Concord Public Library (especially the report for 1861); and my essay on the Concord School of Philosophy, which ran from 1879 to 1888, when Alcott, the Dean of this adult summer school, died ("The Concord School of Philosophy," *New England Quarterly*, Vol. II [1929], pp. 199–233).

Emerson's tribute to Alcott appeared in Appleton's *New American Cyclopedia* (the edition of 1858). A good case can be made (cf. Sanborn and Harris, *op. cit.*) that the portions of the last chapter of Emerson's *Nature*, attributed to "a certain poet," are a version of Alcott, who held the Plotinian view of the Lapse, while Emerson was early an Evolutionist.

Beside Alcott, there were two other nineteenth-century American Neo-Platonists — Dr. Hiram K. Jones, of Jacksonville, Illinois, a lecturer at the Concord School, and Thomas Johnson of Osceola, Missouri, editor of *The* [Neo-] *Platonist*. In the dedication of his *Three Treatises of Plotinus* (1880), Johnson addressed Alcott as "one of the brightest of Heaven's exiles straying from the orb of light."

EMERSON, PREACHER TO HIMSELF

One 'main line' in Emerson's thought, prior to his Unitarian ordination and during his brief pastorate of the Second Church of Boston (cf. his *Journals*, Vols. I and II) is his search for a 'natural religion' — a religion of which the First Principles should be self-evident.

Like Pascal and many another, he revolted against such 'evidences' for the Christian faith as were not religious evidences but logical, historical, scientific. (Cf. Rev. Prof. C. C. J. Webb's *Pascal's Philosophy of Religion.*)

Like Fénelon and many another, he also revolted against a religion in which the rewards and punishments are not religious. Deriding popular eschatology in "Compensation" and elsewhere, he maintains virtue and sanctity to be their own and entirely adequate rewards.

After withdrawing from the ministry, Emerson became a lay preacher with a special mission to intellectuals living in a commercial world and to the young, who must at all costs preserve their idealism. "The American Scholar," delivered at Harvard College in 1837, is but the first of Emerson's exhortations to his special audience of 'clerks,' clerics: in a now outmoded style he commonly calls them "scholars." At Dartmouth, in 1838, he spoke on "Literary Ethics"; at Colby College, in 1841, on "The Method of Nature"; at Colby, in 1863, on "The Man of Letters"; at the University of Virginia, in 1878, on "The Scholar," taking to task the intellectuals for their cowardice, their lack of faith in ideas and ideals. As he had earlier (1854) said to the Adelphi Union of Williams College, "this atheism of the priest, this prose in the poet, this cowardice and succumbing before material greatness, is a treason one knows not how to excuse. Let the scholar stand by his order."

Contradictory judgments of Emerson were passed, during his life, by judges I respect — for example, the elder Henry James and Father Taylor. I see the point of James's adverse verdict, based on what Emerson had *not* gone through: as William says in his *Varieties of Religious Experience*, the Concordian was of the spiritually "once-born." But I share Father Taylor's baffled charity: I cannot deny the saintliness of the man. The sins Emerson had to overcome were fear and nonparticipation in interpersonal communion — and he overcame them. He won his own salvation.

For my 'facts' I have chiefly used Emerson's *Journals* and the equilibrated *Memoir of Emerson* by the philosopher, the assistant of Emerson in his senility, James Elliot Cabot (1887); but, out of the remaining copious richness, I desire to cite *Talks with Ralph Waldo Emerson*, by Charles J. Woodbury (1890), the journals of a Williams College undergraduate whose friendship was with an aging Emerson, and Santayana's "Emerson"

THE SOURCES

in *Interpretations of Poetry and Religion* (1900), and Henry Nash Smith's "Emerson's Problem of Vocation" (*New England Quarterly*, March, 1939).

FÉNELON AMONG THE ANGLO-SAXONS

There have always been oecumenical Swedenborgians, both within and without the Church of the New Jerusalem (founded after the death of Swedenborg, as the Wesleyan, or Methodist, Church was permitted to come into being only after the death of that great Anglican saint, the Rev. John Wesley). In 1853, the Rev. A. E. Ford, a New-Church clergyman, published at Boston the work of Fénelon's friend, Mme Guyon, *Spiritual Torrents* . . . *With Parallel Passages from the Writings of Emanuel Swedenborg*. Dr. W. H. Holcombe of New Orleans, influenced by the French Quietists, published both a volume of *Spiritual Letters* (1885) and a book, somewhat on the order of Coventry Patmore's *The Rod, the Root, and the Flower*, called *Aphorisms of the New Life*, with appendices paralleling Swedenborg, Fénelon, and Mme Guyon: a book which, for its mysticism and literary merit should be reprinted.

The Unitarian clergyman and poet, Jones Very, of Salem (1813–1880) was surely a Quietist (cf., for example his sonnets, "The Idler," "The Hand and Foot," "The Disciple"). In *Maule's Curse* (1938), Yvor Winters, celebrating Very, attributes his Quietism to Puritan and Quaker influence. But Very is far closer to Fénelon. His productive period of writing — 1837–39 — was preceded by Mrs. Follen's *Selections from Fenelon* (1829), designed primarily for Unitarian readers and favorably reviewed by Wm. Ellery Channing in the same year, while Very's first book (which Emerson edited) was not published till 1839.

The Rev. James Freeman Clarke, an oecumenical Unitarian of Boston said [as he is quoted in W. P. Andrews's 1883 edition of *Poems by Jones Very*]: "Mr. Very . . . maintains, as did Fénelon, Mme. Guion, and others, that all sin consists in self-will, all holiness in unconditional surrender of our own will to the will of God. He believes that one whose object is not to do his own will in anything, but constantly to obey God, is led by Him and taught of Him in all things."

NEW ENGLAND SAINTS

"FATHER'S IDEAS": THE ELDER HENRY JAMES

Henry James, Senior, father of the philosopher William and the novelist Henry, tried, at his sons' request, to write his spiritual autobiography but found "egotistic analysis" so distasteful that he could not persist with it. What he managed to write, "Immortal Life: Illustrated in a Brief Autobiographic Sketch of the late Stephen Dewhurst," is included in his son William's first book, *The Literary Remains of the Late Henry James* (ed. William James, 1885).

The elder James was a voluminous and richly styled writer, the chief of the considerable (and engaging) adherents of Swedenborg who — like the Anglican Rev. John Clowes — remained in their original communions or who, like James and Tulk, refusing to believe that their teacher meant to establish a sect, remained isolate. Cf. James's brilliant *The Church of Christ not an Ecclesiasticism: A Letter of Remonstrance to a Member of the Soi-disant New Church* (New York, 1854).

Of James's subsequent books, especially to be recommended are *The Secret of Swedenborg* . . . (1869) and *Society the Redeemed Form of Man and Earnest of God's Omnipotence in Human Nature* . . . (1879).

The interpretations of James's philosophy most useful (*me judice*) are the two small books by his approximate contemporaries and disciples, *The Philosophy of Henry James* by Julia A. Kellogg (1883) and *Swedenborg's Service to Philosophy* by Samuel C. Eby (1891), to which should be added William James's extensive Introduction to the *Literary Remains* (1885) and Ralph Barton Perry's "Religion Versus Morality According to the Elder Henry James," *International Journal of Ethics*, Vol. XLII (1932), pp. 289–303. A more recent study is Frederic H. Young's *The Philosophy of Henry James, Sr.* (New York, 1951).

"Father's ideas" is the phrase of the younger Henry, whose *Notes of a Son and Brother* (1914) commemorates a father and an elder brother whose speculative minds the novelist (possessed of a mind "too fine to be violated by an idea") never comprehended but ever held in affectionate awe. Henry, his mother's child, as William was his father's (increasingly so after the father's death), attributes his phrase to his mother, for whom also the "ideas" were precious not as intelligible but as the

Shekinah of the family: "The happiest household pleasantry invested our mother's fond habit of address, 'Your father's *ideas*, you know — .' " Not what "father's ideas" were but the sense and the presence of his ideas pervade Chapter VI of Henry's *Notes*.

FATHER TAYLOR, or, METAPHOR AMONG THE METHODISTS

The rich and unique source of my life of Taylor is *Father Taylor, the Sailor Preacher. Incidents and Anecdotes of Rev. Edward T. Taylor, 1829–71, For over Forty Years Pastor of the Seaman's Bethel, Boston*, by Hon. Rev. Gilbert Haven . . . and Hon. Thomas Russell, collector of the Port of Boston (1871).

Of the two stanzas of hymns quoted (both included in the *Methodist Hymn Book* published in 1849), the former comes from Dr. Isaac Watts (No. 243) and the latter (No. 219) from the Rev. Charles Wesley.

C. E. NORTON, APOSTLE TO THE GENTILES

My essay is based chiefly on the admirable *Letters of Charles Eliot Norton, with Biographical Comment* by his daughter Sara Norton and M. A. DeWolfe Howe (1913) — a life in letters; Norton's best book.

A descendant of Anne Bradstreet, the son of Andrews Norton, Professor at the Harvard Divinity School, the cousin of President Charles Eliot, who appointed him in 1873 to Harvard's first professorship of the History of Art, a chair which he occupied for twenty-three years, Norton was worthy of his lineage: he abounded in friendships; in astute criticism of American 'democracy'; in educating the young by example as well as precept; in faith and all good works.

At the celebration of his eightieth birthday, Professor George Herbert Palmer admirably said of his teaching: "The methods of Mr. Norton were superbly out of date in our specialistic time."

Norton's publications (of which I give a symptomatic list), testify to his range of sympathies and his humility: *The New Life [Vita Nuova] of Dante; An Essay with Translations* (1859); *Church-Building in the Middle Ages: Venice, Siena, Florence*

NEW ENGLAND SAINTS

(1880); *The Divine Comedy of Dante* ... (1891–92); *The Heart of Oak Books* (six volumes of the world's literature selected and edited for the young: 1894–95); *Letters of James Russell Lowell* (1894); *The Poems of John Donne* ... *with a Preface, and Introduction, and Notes* (1895); *The Poems of Anne Bradstreet* ... *with an Introduction* (1897); *Letters of John Ruskin to Charles Eliot Norton, Selected and Edited* ... (1904); *Longfellow; a Sketch of his Life* ... (1907).

Worth reading as obituaries (that is, recollections of *der alte* Norton) are "A Self-Indulgent Apostle," in Rollo Walter Brown's *Harvard Yard in the Golden Age* (1948), and "Charles Eliot Norton," in *Memories and Milestones* (1915), a 'Lives of the Saints' written by John Jay Chapman — a saint writing about saints, himself not the least of them.

IRVING BABBITT

Many scholar-professors are, upon their retirement or after it, honored by a *Festschrift* composed of various articles — commonly located in the scholar's field. But I know two or three 'saints' lives' of great teachers. One of them is *Irving Babbitt: Man and Teacher*, edited by Frederick Manchester and Odell Shepard (New York, 1941), and admirably prefaced by Babbitt's widow. The book is composed of thirty-nine memoirs. The contributors cover Babbitt's whole career as a teacher and are as varied in their points of view as Babbitt's range might be expected to produce. Notable are the essays by W. F. Giese, K. T. Mei (Professor of Chinese at Harvard), the Rev. James Luther Adams of the Chicago Divinity School, G. R. Elliott of Amherst, Victor M. Hamm of Marquette, Brooks Otis (editor in his Harvard days of the superior 'little' magazine, *The New Frontier*), and Paul Elmer More. Of his old friend, More (pp. 332–33) says: "He was much closer to Buddhism than would appear from his public utterances."

Humanism and America, pro-'Humanist' essays edited by Norman Foerster (1930), was followed in the same year by *The Critique of Humanism*, edited by Hartley Grattan, less an attack than a corrective to a supposed dogmatism. Many of the 'critics' had, indeed, large shared ground with Babbitt: I think particularly of Eliot, Allen Tate, Kenneth Burke, and Yvor

190

THE SOURCES

Winters. Winters, (*Critique*, p. 332), though asserting that there is little in Babbitt which could not be found "in a richer form" in Arnold — a judgment which I would exactly reverse — concedes that "Mr. Babbitt's reiteration of certain ethical values has probably had its effect, however, and where it has influenced such younger men as R. P. Blackmur, Francis Fergusson, Robert Penn Warren, T. S. Eliot, Allen Tate, and others — men who can incorporate these values with a richer experience, the influence, in so far as it may have been at work, is doubtless good."

Four discussions of Babbitt written in the 1940's, and judicial in tone are R. P. Blackmur's "Humanism and Symbolic Imagination: Notes on Re-Reading Irving Babbitt" (*Southern Review*, Autumn, 1941); F. I. Carpenter's "The Genteel Tradition: A Reappraisal" (*New England Quarterly*, Sept., 1942); Wylie Sypher's "Babbitt: A Reappraisal" (*New England Quarterly*, March, 1941); and F. O. Matthiessen's essay-review of *Man and Teacher* (*New England Quarterly*, March, 1942, reprinted in his *Responsibilities of the Critic* [1952], pp. 161–65).

The 'saint's life' most comparable to *Babbitt: Man and Teacher* is *F. O. Matthiessen (1902–1950): A Collective Portrait*, edited by Paul M. Sweezy and Leo Huberman (New York, 1950).

The most philosophically able work on Babbitt remains that of the Swedish scholar, Folke Leander, whose *Humanism and Naturalism* (1937) was doctorally sponsored by Ernst Cassirer.

JOHN BROOKS WHEELWRIGHT

Son of an architect, whose Pepper Pot Bridge yet handsomely conveys Boston's combined subway and elevated across the Charles from Boston to Cambridge, Wheelwright was an architectural historian of distinction, whose taste, transcending Georgian ('Colonial') limitations, rejoiced in the early experiments of nineteenth-century architecture — even pre-Richardson Romanesque and pre-Cram Gothic: the Cowley Fathers' Church on Bowdoin Street and yet more the massive churches which, in the 1860's, were reared in the South End — the social precursor of the 'made land' of the Back Bay — churches like the still extant Billings' Tremont Street Church and Parker's Shawmut Church — a fortress, "high shouldered, round arched, and rigid in outline, with a tall campanile on the corner — the first fruit, so far as Boston was concerned, of the teachings of Ruskin" (Cummings, in the chapter on architecture in Vol. IV of the unsuperseded *Memorial History of Boston* [1881]).

Wheelwright's history has never been published, as it should, whether completed or not. Of his learned and brilliantly insighted essays from the putative history I shall cite "Richard Upjohn, Churchman and Architect," which appeared in the September 1939 issue of the *New England Quarterly* (Vol. XII, pp. 500–509). I suppose that only Henry-Russell Hitchcock, Richardson's monographer, could possibly equal it.